Praise for Bob Litwin and *Live the Best Story of Your Life*

By using his unique coaching method, Bob was able to not only climb from being an ordinary player to being a World Champion but also he has taken his powerful teachings off the court in order to make an even greater impact in the world of business and life.

> —Billie Jean King, 39-time Grand Slam Champion, author of *Pressure is a Privilege*

Bob Litwin's written a wonderful book about how to get more out of life and be happier. He suggests "storytelling" as a route to personal growth. His approach seems impossibly simple, but it is informed by years of work, practice, and living a full life as a husband, father, champion tennis pro and corporate coach. The message is that we need to change the stories we've been telling ourselves about who we are, and replace them with stories about who we hope to become. This is a very original and user-friendly book, with dozens of anecdotes about the author and the people with whom he's worked. From mindfulness to gratitude journals to mentors to naps, Litwin coaches us through this process with enthusiasm and optimism.

> —Barbara Benedek, Screenwriter (*The Big Chill, Pretty Woman, Sabrina*)

Two things have guided me to become the person I want to be: mountain climbing and Bob Litwin's New Story model. Bob's brand of storytelling has helped me achieve as a mountaineer, business professional and family man. Most people won't climb Everest, but anyone can do the simple work of *Live the Best Story of Your Life* and become exactly who they want to be.

> —Bo Parfet, author of *Die Trying: One Man's Quest to Conquer the Seven Summits*, co-founder of Jumar Management and Denali Venture Philanthropy

Bob Litwin and his teachings changed my tennis story, which, in turn, changed my life story. His coaching made me more patient, and more grateful—and for that, I'm eternally grateful to him.

> —Gerald Marzorati, award-winning author of *Late to the Ball* and former editor of the New York Times Magazine

Unbelievably effective, and everyone *can* do it. Instantaneous change and you don't even need to leave the office.

—Joel Greenblatt, *New York Times* bestselling author of
The Little Book that Beats the Market

Bob is a very special human being. Wish more of planet Earth had his stuff. He is simply the best!

—Jim Loehr, *New York Times* bestselling author of *Power of Full Engagement*, co-founder of Johnson and Johnson Human Performance Institute

I have worked closely with some of the world's greatest professional, Olympic, and collegiate coaches of elite athletes. Bob Litwin ranks among the best. His Tao and Zen-techniques allow you to discover and unlock the extraordinary powers of body, mind, and spirit for dramatic improvement—not only in your tennis game, but in all arenas of your life. Your game will never be the same once you commit to the Litwin's method of ageless wisdom and practical strategy.

—Jerry Lynch, Ph.D., author of *Thinking Body, Dancing Mind*

What's your story? We all have one...*Live the Best Story of Your Life* offers a simple yet powerful and practical story system/methodology which will empower the reader to initiate positive changes and live their dream. Throughout the book, Litwin shares his personal experiences and stories of his clients, continually encouraging his readers to throw out their old, negative story and usher in a new story. The 33 personal coaching sessions help the reader to build "their spine" and foundation to lasting growth. I recommend this book to anyone who is looking for inspiration and wants to live the best story of their life.

—Rob Polishook, performance coach and author of *Inside the Zone: 32 Mental Training Workouts for Champions*

Throw out every book you've ever bought on change. Here is the silver bullet. The single most important book you will ever read, guaranteed to make you feel limitless in business, create bliss in your personal life and dramatically shift your idea of what you are capable of. The best part? It's easy! Let Bob Litwin change your life.

—Jay Goldman, founder and CEO, J. Goldman & Co.

Bob Litwin's book is a remarkable gift for anyone looking for enduring happiness even in the face of self-doubt, fear or despair. As a turnaround specialist, Litwin's compelling story of personal triumph and his secret sauce coaching skills have helped thousands of people live the best stories of their lives. This book is the game-changer that can put you on the fast track to a life well lived and incredible, long-lasting success.

—P.J. Simmons, co-founder of Corporate Eco Forum,
founder of The Tennis Congress and co-author of
The Green to Gold Business Playbook

Bob's model takes the fear out of making big changes and his storytelling technique is a commonsense, basic approach that everyone can use. *Live the Best Story of Your Life* has helped many of us thrive in difficult markets, deepen our personal relationships, and dramatically improve our health and fitness. Change is easy!

—Mike Marrale, Managing Dir., Head of Research, Sales &
Trading, Investment Technology Group

Bob opened my eyes to what it truly means to be successful in every aspect of my life: professional, marriage, family, friendships, and health. Through teaching me the skills of "story writing", Bob has taught me how to visually and mentally create a new path to reach my full potential. As a result, I have seen monumental leaps in both my professional and personal life. My only regret is that I did not meet Bob until my adult life. His desire to share his experience and knowledge through *Live the Best Story of Your Life* is truly a gift to anyone who wants to take their life to the next level.

—Eric Wasserman, hedge fund portfolio manager

My initial conversation with Bob was one of the most profoundly life-altering conversations I've ever had. He so effortlessly showed me the version of myself that I had been searching for and helped point me in the direction I've always wanted to go, but couldn't. My old life story was just too much in the way, and now Bob has given me the tools to focus on my new story. *Live the Best Story of Your Life* is the guidebook that will change the life of anyone looking for more.

—Klinton Kraft, Partner, Digital Blue

Like a fine wine, full-bodied, robust, with much of the depth and scope of his life experiences blended into to a unique flavor of a person that he has become, Bob is a coach that we all can savor. *Live the Best Story of Your Life* is an extraordinary vintner. His model for making changes is nothing short of miraculous.

—Fred McNair, President of McNair and Co.,
Rrench Open Champion

For anyone who has ever felt miserable, desperate and felt that things were impossible, Bob's new story method is the answer. From sleep to losing weight to leaving dead end relationships, the New Story method will turn it all around. *Live the Best Story of Your Life* is about soaring in business, building incredible relationships and enjoying every single step of the journey. The book is the path to a life of authenticity, courage and true joy.

—Laura Jacobs, founder of Jacobs Management Group, Inc.

Beyond strategy, Bob teaches us the power of transforming the stories within us for success in sport, business, and relationships. In this book, Bob empowers us with the technology for abundance and happiness in life.

—Phil Wharton, author of *The Wharton Health Series*

By working with Bob I have become much more confident in myself as a runner and in my ability to attack any challenges, mental or physical. In the Steeplechase final at the World Junior Championships in Barcelona, Spain this summer, I changed as a competitor. I was only using stories that helped me to run fast, I let go of negative thoughts and I wasn't nervous before the race. Having a positive story has helped me do my best in any situation and allows me to be happier and more successful in my life.

—Brianna Nerud, Oregon Varsity Track, two-time member of
the USA World Junior Championship team

Bob's teachings are genuine and sincere because he has taught and developed them himself; so he has "lived" the reality and "walked the walk". It's a dream come true to be exposed to Bob at any level.

—Ed Schroback, Vietnam veteran and USTA tournament player

LIVE
THE BEST
STORY
OF YOUR
LIFE

LIVE

THE BEST
STORY
OF YOUR

LIFE

A WORLD CHAMPION'S GUIDE
TO LASTING CHANGE

BOB LITWIN

Improve your life. Change your world.

Improve your life. Change your world.

Hatherleigh Press is committed to preserving and protecting the natural resources of the earth. Environmentally responsible and sustainable practices are embraced within the company's mission statement.

Visit us at www.hatherleighpress.com and register online for free offers, discounts, special events, and more.

Live the Best Story of Your Life
Text copyright © 2016 Bob Litwin

Library of Congress Cataloging-in-Publication Data is available upon request.
ISBN: 978-1-57826-632-6

Interior Design by Cynthia Dunne
Author Photograph by Bill Jellick

Printed in the United States
10 9 8 7 6 5 4 3

Dedication

To Carol who, just by being Carol, showed me living the best story of my life was always possible, in good and difficult times, in victory and defeat, in joy and sadness, in both love and loss. That there is always light that shines through darkness. Her light shines on as I continue to live the best story of my life.

Contents

Foreword

Bob Litwin is an extraordinary tennis player. He has won dozens of U.S. National Championships in both singles and doubles, as well as a World Championship. For over 25 years, I've had the privilege of taking private lessons from Bob. Just think about that. Almost every week, getting to hit and play sets with one of the world's greatest players—and for more than 25 years! (Okay, that also means losing every week for over two decades, but still!)

It's just that, as it turns out, for all those years spent on the court, I wasn't really taking tennis lessons. Of course, in some sense I was. But in pretty short order, I began to realize that tennis was just a vehicle for the real learning. What does it take to keep improving? To be in the moment? To stay focused? To understand your mission? To redefine "winning"? (Believe me—that one came in handy!) To overcome adversity? To change your story? To write a new story? And how can you do it right now? Not next month. Not next week. Now.

I'm an investment fund manager by profession and I think about the lessons I've learned on the court from Bob pretty much every day. What story should I tell myself after a tough day? A good one? Regardless of what's happening in the market, how do I stay in the moment when I have a meeting with a client or co-worker; how do I disregard what I can't affect right now, and focus on what's important, the task at hand? How do I come up with a new plan, a new story, when things aren't working the way I'd like?

Sure, to be the best in the world (or even the best in the nation) in anything, you need to be in some way extraordinary, even extreme in some ways. And Bob has both of these qualities. So you might think that methods that have worked for Bob, have no relevance for "normal" people. After all, Bob's a world champion who advises world class athletes, hedge fund managers, and titans of industry, so these people seem to be doing pretty well already. In other words, you might assume that his teachings and methods might not work for everyone.

But here's the thing. Bob didn't start out as a champion. In fact, just the opposite. He didn't even play college tennis for his alma mater, the University of Michigan. (On his first week at school, the coach sent him over to hit with one of the Varsity players. Bob was demolished so thoroughly, he quit right there. Of course, that Varsity player went on to win the National Collegiate Championship, but Bob didn't know that...at that point, he was just a pretty good tennis player without the right attitude or game plan.)

So, here's the good news. The real secret isn't starting out as a champion. Almost no one does. The real secret is constantly working at it, wanting to improve, always getting a little better, or trying again. Take your current circumstances and write a new story that gets you to the next step. It's unbelievably effective and everyone can do it.

While reading this book, I could hear Bob's voice on every page. In fact, I hear Bob's encouraging and inspiring voice in my head every day. After reading this book, I know that you will too. For that gift, we are both incredibly lucky. Not that most of us will end up as world champions, but every one of us can get better and do better, and with Bob's help, we can all keep working to live the best story of our lives.

—Joel Greenblatt

Joel Greenblatt is an American academic, hedge fund manager, investor, best-selling author, adjunct professor at the Columbia University Graduate School of Business, and Founder of Gotham Capital.

PART I

Out with the Old Story, in with the New

CHAPTER 1

The Story That Changed My Life

At the heart of every winter, there is a
quivering spring; and behind the veil of each
night there is a smiling dawn.

—Kahlil Gibran

I n the spring of 2008, I watched my soulmate of 28 years lose
her three-year battle with cancer. Two months later the hip
surgery I'd gotten less than a year before failed, and I was at risk
for a massive fracture. I'd been the #1 senior tennis player in the
world, and now, if I stepped off a curb, I might find myself in
the hospital, a hospital that contained devastating memories. It
sounded like my competitive playing days were over. I was so
wrung out from losing Carol, I was sure I couldn't go through
surgery again. And who would take care of me when I got home?
But keeping my hip meant living with the pain for the rest of

my life. I felt old, alone, and afraid. Nothing seemed to be going right. For the first time in my life, I wanted to give up.

And then on the morning of Carol's first birthday after her death, I'd stayed in bed for as long as I could before I got up and rinsed my face, and when I looked in the mirror, I heard her voice very clearly. "Bob, what would you tell a client?" Like a blast in the brain, the answer was clear: *I needed a New Story!*

So, I sat at my computer and I wrote a New Story. Not a story of where I was. I'd been telling that story enough. But a New Story of where I wanted to be in my life.

I am young. I am strong. I am not alone. I have friends and family who will be with me. My house is comfortable. I have the inspirational memory of Carol pushing through chemo and radiation. I have gone through surgery and rehab once, and I can do it again. I am a master of rehab. The surgery will be a step to full health. My middle name is resilience and I will be back on the tennis court within three months. I will be competing again. I love the challenge of dealing with adversity. I am a model for those around me in pushing through difficult experiences. I will grow from this experience. I am overflowing with life. I am a vessel for love. I have had one angel in my life, I will find another.

A New Story. A *better* story. A story of hope. A story of yes. A story of optimism. A story of proactivity. A story that inspired me. A story that worked. A story that I could start moving toward, one step at a time.

I came alive. I started calling different docs for second and third opinions. Within a week, I'd decided on the hospital, surgeon, the type of hip replacement, and I had booked a surgery date. I'd arranged for family and friends to stay with me for two weeks post-op, when I couldn't be alone. As the day got closer, I was actually excited. I was totally jacked up and ready. No fear. No doubt. No worry. Moving away from my Old Story, toward my New Story.

Within a year it was clear my surgery was a success; I was back on the court and accelerating into the most exciting chapter of my life. I had more clients than ever, my work on Wall Street was exploding, I was a finalist in a national championship, had been inducted into the Eastern Tennis Hall of Fame, and I'd met a new angel with whom I would share my life. I had written the story and now I was living it.

You are about to get a gift . . . this gift is going to come in the form of a special skill.

One that, if you practice it and get good at it, will lead you where you want to go and help you change any area of your life. (Well, it can't change your eye color or your foot size but anything else). The skill is something you've done all your life and never really thought about: the simple act of storytelling.

You probably picked up this book because there's something you want that you don't have: a way to be, act, perform, something you wish you could do. A way you think or believe, an attitude you have that you know doesn't work for you. This book is going to take you to a new version of you, using the simple process of storytelling. You decide who you want to be, and this brand of storytelling gets you there. Once you learn it, you can be or change or do anything. I went from never winning tournaments to being the best in the world in tennis, from being a junior high history teacher to coaching others to reach heights they never imagined. And you can do whatever you want, too.

So strap yourself in. Give me your attention. No smartphone, tablet, or computer screen. I am talking to the part of you that isn't in the daily grind. The part of you not operating from your deeply conditioned mind. That mind doesn't want you to change. What wants to change is you. The inner you. The you that knows there must be a better way, a different way. This book is the better way, a culmination of 40 years in the field of human potential.

Your potential.

The material in this book has created world champions out of club athletes, seen Wall Street hedge funders make tens of millions for their firms, put out-of-work actors back on Broadway, helped powerful CEOs have better relationships with their spouses, led stay-at-home moms to days that are free of anguish and much more.

The popularity of the work is due to its central tenet, something we are inextricably drawn to and do without realizing: Storytelling. From the first drawings in the Lascaux Caves in 13000 bce to Gilgamesh and the stone pillars to Shakespeare and J. K. Rowling, storytelling has been a fascination and a survival mechanism. Without fully realizing it, the act of storytelling rules our lives. Change your story? Change your life. Though brain science has confirmed it, and the best and brightest understand this, the question remains: How?

This book is the how. *Live the Best Story of Your Life* harnesses the power of the story, shining the light on hidden stories that hold us back, providing the foolproof guide to new stories and giving you 33 coaching sessions that make that New Story stick. These sessions provide you with a full-time live-in coach, who applauds your successes, pushes you whenever you need it, and provides a lifeline when you find yourself backsliding. *Live the Best Story of Your Life* does not shift what we do, it shifts who we are. It is a prodigious almost magical experience that starts the moment we see adversity as a story, rather than a truth. A compact, substantive read, it's written so you can use it as a repeated guide throughout your life. Whether you are on Wall Street, in a classroom, at clubs and tournaments, or trying to raise a family, if you are hungry for lasting change, this is for you.

Using this method, a bond trader kicked a million-dollar field goal in front of 60,000 people. A high school middle-distance runner ran the fastest girl's scholastic mile, had ten personal bests, became the county and state champion and an All American. A CEO lost 40 pounds, broke up with her (separated but not divorced) boyfriend and started the business of her dreams. A deeply depressed out-of-shape dentist who was ready to end his life is now expanding his practice and has started training five days a week to run four marathons in four months to raise money for a suicide prevention hotline.

What do they have in common? All of them used storytelling to get what they wanted. And you can, too. One after the other, the most successful people in their fields are getting clear on their stories, finding it easy to achieve their goals, and living their dreams.

It's simple: Know where you are starting. Decide where you want to go.

What is your story? What is the Old Story you want to jettison and the New Story you want to live? Don't know? This book will help you find out. Let's explore together.

Get ready to enjoy the ride.

What do you have to lose?

CHAPTER 2

How to Make Change Easy

Failure is not fatal, but failure to change
might be.

—JOHN WOODEN

H ow would your life be different if you believed this simple
thought:

Change is easy.

How many times have you heard people say change is hard?
Change is painful. We are conditioned to believe we have to stay
the same—that change doesn't last. We are told small changes
don't matter: an Old Story we've been sold for years. If we really
want change in our lives, this story doesn't work. What if you
were told you could alter that story?

You can. In fact, any story can be changed. I know this because
I wasn't always a world champion. At one time, I was in a dead

end, low self-esteem job, feeling like hired help for people I perceived had more and were more than me. On the court, I was losing to players who were less skilled than I was.

Financially, I was struggling, borrowing money for a down payment and driving a Volkswagen Beetle with a hole in the floor. My marriage was going downhill, and my 60-plus-hour work week left me no time for the people and activities I loved. On Father's Day I found myself running the parent-child tournament rather than being with my own kids.

I wanted more. I wanted more as a father. I wanted more from my marriage. I wanted more on the court. And I wanted more in my career. How did I begin to make dramatic changes in every area of my life? I wrote a different story. And change became an exciting and yes, even at times, an easy journey.

Less than a year after writing that first New Story, I was winning tennis tournaments, I had gotten divorced, met an angel, and started to create the groundwork for The Focused Game Method that got me off the court to working with private clients, where I could set my own schedule and reach my financial goals. Since then I've gone from being a player who couldn't win to the #1 ranked player in the world, eight-time member of the US Senior Davis Cup, winner of the Maccabian Gold Medal and inductee into the Eastern Tennis Hall of Fame. On top of that I began working as a coach for one of the most consistently successful hedge funds on Wall Street, showing traders and analysts how new stories can help them keep their heads on straight as a means to higher performance. My clients now include some of the biggest business influencers and media moguls in the country.

No matter how big your ambition, how small your wish, how wild your goal, how seemingly futile your dream—this two-step process from your Old Story to your New Story will get you there. You may be asking: *But how can I know this really works? What if I waste my time? Maybe it worked for you, but stuff like this never works for me, I'm just going to be disappointed again. I can't change this about myself, I've never been able to, and this book is no different. Change is too hard, and it takes too long.*

Stop. Take a deep breath. The story we've been sold on change is about to change. You don't have to have an adversarial relationship with it anymore. Change has a bad reputation. But it doesn't have to be hard. The truth is, change is always going on. Even when you are you're sleeping it's happening. In fact there is nothing in the world that isn't changing—right now, as you read, in this moment and time. And it started small.

When I was lying in bed recovering from hip surgery, the idea of playing the next National Grass Court Championships would have seemed like a huge change. But just by writing an Old Story about my health that was not working and writing a new one that might, I started to change. By using some of the most fantastic tools passed down from mentors and experts, I became, again, the national champion.

You have already changed just from reading the first few pages of this book because you now know what is possible. There is a way out of old thinking and beliefs that have kept you where you don't want to be. The New Story is your new life. You can start moving toward it. Right now.

Change is right brained. It's creative, intuitive, instinctive. Change is not linear. It's iterative. Once you've opened the door through observing yourself . . . you are a different person. The door won't ever close completely. And you will never be the same.

Change happens on a level we cannot grasp anymore than our ancestors couldn't grasp that the world was round. But as you read this book, just by taking small steps, you will begin to notice a remarkable shift.

A trader I've been working with for a while said the other day, "I used to drink when a trade didn't go well. Now I want to, but I don't." How did that happen? He wrote a New Story. A better story of who he aspired to be. Someday, if this trader keeps working on his Old and New Stories, he won't even think about having a drink. And soon a trade he used to label as "bad" will feel like an opportunity. You often can't see your own growth because you're in it. You can only see it by looking back. *I used to be that. Now I am this.*

A portfolio manager who was losing money, told a New Story about managing his team, and by the end of the year had made $10 million for his firm.

A high school track star who finished dead last in one of the most important races of her senior year, told a New Story about competition and wound up winning the National Scholastic Mile three months later.

Don't worry if you have always been one way or if you feel like you can't change it. In the act of picking up this book, you have already changed. Trust me that when you do this very first step, you will already be on your way to a cookie-free night, a day without procrastination, racing a zip line over the Amazon, taking a slow walk in the park. Congratulations! You are on your way.

If you go no further than this right now, you have already taken a huge step toward positive change. Too simple? Sorry, you will just have to get used to change being simple, fast, fun, and painless. One day you might even laugh about how you used to think about change. Your New Story about change will be one that works. You'll share it with family and friends. You might share it with the world. On Oprah.

Often this is when the critic's voice arrives. The voice that says, "I don't even want to change. I like myself just the way I am." Hang in there. You don't have to listen to that voice.

This is your life. You get to make the rules. Once you see change as simply a story you tell, the world opens up. Change is happening, even when it seems like it's not. The world of being willing to try new things, of can-do attitudes: I can do anything, I can be anything. You will begin to believe I'm going to do it. It's going to happen.

What do you have to lose?

CHAPTER 3

Carved in Stone, Written in Blood: The No-Quit Contract That Will Save Your Life

> I am the master of my fate: I am the
> captain of my soul.
>
> —NELSON MANDELA

I am asking you to believe something that, at times, may be hard to do: change your story.

When you write the New Story it isn't who you are. It is who you aspire to become. Who you need to become in order to get what you want in your life. When a client writes a New Story they often say, "But that's not who I am." Of course, I know that, and that is why it is called your New Story. Our stories are like our religions, we cling to them. Often we made them up during tough times or trauma to explain what was going on, they helped us survive, no matter if they weren't true. Often they are passed down to us from trusted mentors, parents, coaches, rabbis. The people who passed these stories down were perhaps well intentioned, but somehow, maybe in the way we interpreted the messages, the stories did not work. Maybe the stories, themselves, were misinterpretations of the way we were. As we moved forward in our lives, they tended to grip us with iron fists.

There will be moments you might lose faith. You start to doubt. That's normal. I've been there, many times. At the beginning, almost every time I tried to change, the questions and doubts popped up. That voice is your Old Story talking. The one that wants you to stay the same. When it starts to chatter, it's hard not to listen, so it can help to have something to fall back on that will prop you up, remind you of what the new, soon-to-be you believes. So, right at the outset, sign a contract with yourself. One you can look at when the doubter, skeptic, or critic starts making noise. A deal you make with yourself to get back on track. Refer to it. Use it. It is the commitment you made when you bought this book.

The No-Quit Contract

1. **I am open.** I will leave some things at the door including my skepticism and doubt and the words: someday, should, but, if only, can't, I am trying, nothing is happening. I will stick these in the closet as I do this work. If I want to, I can

go back at the end of the book and pick these up. But while in the world of the book, they will stay on the sidelines. Being open keeps me from going off the rails. When I go off the rails, I can always come back to the contract, read a private coaching chapter, or write another New Story.

2. **I can change.** I trust that change is happening. I am made up of software, not hardware. Everything can be reprogrammed. Change happens without even trying. But when I doubt I can change, I hijack my efforts. Stories like: I've tried, I've tried, and I've failed are replaced by, actually I can change. Everything I think, feel, believe, say and do is a habit, and I can break old habits and create new ones that give me what I want.

3. **Nothing in my past has power over this present moment.** In this moment, the past doesn't matter. It has no power over me. That was yesterday, last year, and has nothing to do with what I can do now. Right now. In this very moment I can think, say, feel, believe anything I want to. This moment can be what I want it to be right now. I get to define how long that is, a second, an hour, a day, or the rest of my life.

4. **I am all in.** "Faith is taking the first step without seeing the whole staircase," Martin Luther King, Jr. tells us. I will operate on blind faith.

What do I have to lose?

Your Signature
Date

So when things get tough, when the old voice of doubt starts to chatter, and you start to think about bailing out . . . reread your contract. It is the voice of where you are going.

CHAPTER 4

The Beast before the Bounty: The Story You Can No Longer Afford to Tell

Living is easy with eyes closed,
misunderstanding all you see.

—JOHN LENNON

When I begin to work with people, I often ask them to tell me those things in their lives they think may be interfering with getting what they want in life. I've heard: I am fearful, I don't take risks, I'm impatient, I doubt myself, I worry about what others think, I am unhealthy, tired, unfocused. Sometimes, in order to get to their story, they share much more.

There's a Wall Street guy, mid-30s, big-time job, with lots of external success, who wrote the story of his past, going back to his childhood. His father was a disenfranchised Vietnam veteran who said to his family, every day, I'm going to Washington to kill the president. This young boy, my client, kept telling his father every day, "You can't do this, we need you." His father was a mailman who got his job done in half the time by hopping over hedges because he had another job; he was a janitor at the kid's school. This kid had to help his father scrape the gum off the student desks.

Before this grown guy wrote his Old Story, that story was still going on for him: *I am alone, I need to work alone, no one else can do it, I can't depend on anyone.* He was working 17 hours a day. He had three groups totaling 45 people working under him, and they gave him three people to help him delegate. Each of the people would be handling 15 people, but he said, Forget it, I don't want anyone else to delegate, I need to be the direct manger of 48 people. He fired those three people.

After our first meeting, I sent him a picture of the Atlas in Rockefeller Center and told him, you're no longer alone. I can lift some of that world for you. Writing out his Old Story helped lift the weight, shedding light on his beliefs and assumptions that were keeping him in an unhealthy, overwhelmed place. After writing the story, he was able to see it from a distance, as if it were someone else's story. He was able to take a good look at it, and to jettison it by dissecting it and seeing the idioms, rules, and laws he'd given himself to live by. By discovering what lay within the Old Story, he was able to move toward living a new one.

Now he has 150 direct reports working under him and he welcomes the help from the assistant managers he allows his wife to support him when he needs a break, he no longer feels alone.

The more deeply we are entrenched in our stories, the more we don't get to live the life that's waiting for us. This chapter is about diving into the Old Story, cutting it up, dissecting it, finding what used to work for us and what no longer works for us. It's the beginning of your journey to living your best stories.

Everyone has some part of their life that they want to improve or change. Something that isn't working—maybe they are too negative or judgmental, high-anxiety, workaholic, lazy, they smoke or eat badly, or cheat on their spouse. We are in a self-help frenzy, the field is growing by 11.5 billion dollars annually. From George Combe's *The Constitution of Man* in the mid-1800s, self-help has seen exponential growth. But what are people looking for? And why is it not working?

The challenge is that people want to fix things before they actually see them. They want to send someone who overeats to the gym to lose weight, they want to tell someone in a failing marriage how to listen better, they want to teach a rageaholic how to meditate. Before we will-power ourselves to a different action, we need to see that when we say "that's the way I am," this story is keeping us where we are. The person who overeats may have a story that eating is how she makes herself feel good. Going to the gym will not solve this. She needs to see that story and get clear that it isn't working. Maybe going to the gym will follow. The person in a failing marriage may feel unworthy, listening may not help him feel worthier. The person who is raging may feel that he is out of control, meditating will not make him feel more in control. We need to see the stories behind our actions before we simply run in and change our behavior and trust that's all it will take.

This process of storytelling helps us see. You may have picked up this book because something is not quite working in your life, you are not getting something that you want. It may feel like a huge ball of wax, or it may feel like there is one niche in your life that needs attention. Whatever it is, start out with the story that you most want to change. It might be, I'm not able to get the best out of the people working for me, I can't move up a level in my tennis, I'm too tired at the end of my day to be engaged with my family. We support those stories and beliefs because we can't always see them. We can't get the distance we need to shift them. The act of storytelling helps us identify them.

We have stories about everything: people cutting in front of us at the market, bad service in restaurants, children's' behavior in public places, people who drive and talk on the phone, about sports, work, intensity, yoga, religion, friends, anxiety, and fear. These stories may have deep roots but that's actually not why we cling to them. We cling to them because we have practiced them for years, become experts at them and we think they are unchangeable.

I have always been a procrastinator. I am known as Mr. Late for the Date. That's the way that I am. I have always been that way. I've tried to change but old habits die hard. Those are indicators of the Old Story. You are not hardwired that way. Actually, what you think, believe, feel, say, and do is software. The Old Story, although uncomfortable for some to write and explore, is actually not hard because it's the life you are already living. No having to make it up. Just take a look. You can even start small. "I never get a break." It's all reprogrammable and changeable. First be aware. Then you will begin to change.

But how do you start?

Pick an area of your life that you'd like to change at least some aspect of. This may include but is not limited to:

Work

Family

Love/Romance

Sports

Money

Health

Community

Awareness

Communication

Write a statement about what's not working in this area. It can help to answer the following questions:

I'm afraid that_____

I can't live a better story around this because_____

The reason I'm not as good as I want to be is _____

I know I can be better and what keeps me from that is _____

_____

I'm the kind of person who_____

I do better when _____

I am at a disadvantage because _____

If I had _____ then I'd be_____

It's hard for me because_____

I haven't achieved this yet because_____

I can never really achieve this because_____

If only _____ were different I could _____

I have always been somebody who thinks _____

I have always been somebody who believes _____

_____ about time.

Try to write the whole truth. If you don't know where to start, you might start with something you say a lot that ends with *that's the way I am*. For instance, *I can only write if I'm on deadline, that's just the way I am.* That's an indicator of where you're stuck. Or you might start with just who you are. *I am a tennis player, and I am not getting the results I want. I tend to get uptight in competition. I am good, but I don't play to my level when I am in pressure situations.* It doesn't have to be an A+ school essay . . . you can use bullet points, partial sentences—perfection is not important.

Here a couple of old stories from people who appear to others to be hugely successful.

David's business puts up huge numbers, he lives in a beautiful home, belongs to the fanciest golf club in town. He started and grew a gigantic wholesale business dealing with paper products. When you first meet him, you might think he's a relaxed family man with the world at his fingertips. But inside that polished exterior was a pretty intense Old Story:

I am a workaholic. I eat, breathe, and sleep work. I started my journey seven years ago with passion, vision and excitement. I felt unstoppable. But as business started to develop and the economic environment got tougher, my attitude changed—and the passion faded. Now everything feels hard. I have started to resent my work and lost the excitement that I once had. I question why I chose this path, and wonder what it would be like had I chosen another. I feel stuck, scared, and uncertain about how things are going to progress. I joke that Billy Joel's "Pressure" is the theme song of my life.

Everyone looks to me for guidance, strength, and direction, and all I want is someone else to follow. I'm the only one who can do it. There isn't enough time in the day. I'm an anxious person. I'm often consumed with competition—either direct competitors or the idea of

*competition. I feel insecure and always assume that the competition
is doing something better. I struggle to enjoy the moment. I'm not
even sure what I'm chasing anymore. I just know that this story is
not the one that I had hoped I would be telling . . .*

Steve is the COO of one of the most well-known financial
institutions in the world. You would never know from his
modest demeanor how big and important he is in the financial
world. He is soft spoken and somewhat withdrawn, but if he
walked into the finest restaurants the owner would clear the
best table for him. He is uncomfortable with people doing for
him just because of his business stature. His reputation is stel-
lar, which is not easy to achieve when working in a world of
power brokers.

His Old Story was filled with parts that were just not working.

*I don't sleep well. I am low on energy. My motivation is low. I
don't bring my best each day. I have not lived up to my potential. I
don't work out consistently. I don't stick with rituals that are good
for me. I lose discipline with my diet. I don't enjoy what I am doing.
I am critical. I am judgmental. I future trip. I am not there for my
son. I don't own my successes. I get upset about small things. I can't
let go of upset. I am not in the present.*

I asked each of them, "Are these stories working for you?"
Before they set their intentions by writing new stories both of
them answered that their stories were not getting them what
they wanted. Your story is what you have been living till now, a
story that you probably didn't make lots of choices about (not
to say that you aren't content with it). You didn't write it before
you lived it.

Write your story.

I know, I make it sound so easy, don't I? But it really can be that simple. You may not believe it, but you're likely dying to tell yourself your own story. Give yourself time, make yourself into an attentive audience, and let the words flow. Don't overthink it. Make it a first draft if you want. You can go back to it or not. No rules here.

Now read it over. What is your story? Can you see stuff in there that keeps you from where you want to go in some part of your life? Maybe being too impatient, pessimistic, angry, righteous. Anything you'd like to get rid of? What about something that isn't there that you'd like to add? Check out the negative beliefs in this story . . . This is what you're using to keep you where you are.

Reread your story a couple of times. Do more ideas pop up? More thoughts? Things you didn't write the first time? Something that doesn't work in your career, at home, with yourself, with your friends? Add them.

Now put down your writing.

Look at it in a couple of hours. See how you feel about it. You might want to add or take something out. Your story might turn out to be about something else entirely. Like you were writing a story about your business and what started to surface in the story was not feeling good about yourself and how much you want to just feel good. Maybe you thought it was about eating too many cookies and what shines through is the desire to be a person with self-discipline. Your world would be different with discipline. It wasn't at all about the cookie.

You have written your Old Story and reread it a bunch, and you know what doesn't work for you, what you want to get rid of, reduce, increase. Just by looking at your Old Story, you are starting to live a new one. You are moving. One of my clients,

Andrea, had a pretty bad story that she was believing, thinking, feeling, talking, and being. She was raising two kids, her back was bad, her husband was working hard and, even though he helped out, it wasn't enough. She wasn't making progress on career plans. She had changed her diet and was exercising a lot to be healthy, to increase energy, and to look better. So she talked this out with me. I listened. That is what I do.

And I said to her what I say to almost anyone who asks for my input: "Write this Old Story, your BS (Bad Story) and watch what happens." So Andrea left and one week later we talked again. "How are you making out with your BS?" She said, "It is weird but when I sat down to write it a couple of days ago, it felt forced to write what I was saying before. The fact that I realized that I was just telling a bad story changed it right away. I was listening to my Old Story rather than seeing that it was just a story. That distance changed me."

Change is happening when you hardly know it. You just need to start with that overused old story.

"So," I told her. "Now go write your New Story."

But what about the New Story? Your vision, who you want to be, and where you want your new trajectory to take you? We need to put that out there so we are moving in that direction, the direction that will give us what we want. The New Story is filled with those things we often don't even dream can be there. Begin to dream.

CHAPTER 5

Welcome to Your Personal Oz: Writing the New Story

If you don't know where you're going, any
path will get you there.

—George Harrison

What if you had the opportunity to actually decide what you want to be, who you are in the world? What if you had a chance to create what you imagine for yourself? People often get stuck and scared right there. They don't know where to start. They tend to identify with material things instead: *I wish I had another relationship. I'd love more money. I want to get that promotion.* The reason they get stuck is that external wishes and dreams are not personal enough. They are "out there." The New Story is not about what you want, it's about who you want to *be*. And it can get scary and exciting when you get away from what you want and think of changing who you actually are. And yet if you shift how you are in the world, you often wind up getting what you want.

Writing your New Story is creative work. This is not about being realistic. Being realistic creates limitations based on your old way of being. It is about writing a story about yourself and your life that is absent of fear and limitations based on old ways of being. However terrifying and exciting, this won't take anything away, it will give you the life you've never before had the audacity to imagine. No more if only's. No more "I wish I could . . ." This is the story of what can be. A story of optimism. A story of YES!

How do you start?

Look at your Old Story again and make a list of those things that, if you had your way, wouldn't be there. Your New Story might be the opposite of some of the things in the original version of your story. You adjust some things, you get rid of others. You add brand new things.

When you write your New Story, you write it in the present tense.

Your Old Story might look like this: *I'm overwhelmed, I don't delegate responsibility well, when a competitor starts to do something I'm not doing, it makes me uptight.* Your New Story might start: *I'm relaxed under pressure. I am able to delegate responsibility well, when my competitors do something I'm not doing, it challenges me and makes me a better at my business.*

If your Old Story is, *I've always been anxious,* the New Story might be: *I'm a master of managing my anxiety.*

If that critic voice pops up and says, "Hold it, that's not what I am," stop and take a deep breath. Of course you are not the New Story yet. This is where you are headed, it's the life that's calling out to you.

Write with no fear, not being sensible, not worrying about if you can. This is the story of your future of possibilities. And the horizon can be very wide.

My own New Story was about freedom, security, health, loving and being loved, having fun, being young in spirit, doing something that makes a difference in the world, being a positive model for change, being free of mental anguish, having balance and meaningful relationships, being committed to growing my spirit self, competing like a champion, living in the present. You may just be trying to make ends meet, get to work on time, put food on the table, drive home in time to connect with your kids.

Fortunately, just because you are living hand-to-mouth doesn't mean you can't have a New Story. One stressed-out banker told me that a part of him wished he were laid off in the job crisis so that he could sit back and reevaluate what he was doing with his life.

Why wait until you are laid off or for there to be some tough catalyst?

Write your story now.

Write your New Story now, while you are living your current story.

Remember David and his Old Story? Here is the new one that he wrote:

I maintain a healthy work-life balance. When working I am there 100 percent. When I walk through my door at home I am a totally engaged father and husband. I work in a state of focus, loving the ease and the difficulties that come my way. The harder things are the deeper my focus. I jump out of bed every day eager to do battle with the challenges of work. I never look back. I have no regrets. I am fearless about the uncertainty of industry. The theme of my life is "pressure is a privilege." I love to mentor those who look to me and I am able to reach out to those who have traveled the path before me. I learn every day. I manage my time effectively. I reduce anxiety instantly when I start to feel it. Competition raises my work game. I enjoy my life. I live in the present. I am living the story of my life.

Which do you think stood a better chance of getting David living his best story? The tired old negative one or the new one that is filled with positivity, proactivity, newness, and life? Well, he started to take steps into becoming what he had written, and now, less than one year later, he has dinner at home with his family almost every night, he is exercising five days a week, his business had increased by 30 percent while his anxiety has dropped to a rare moment. He invested in bringing a full-time coach into his business so that he can continue to grow his personal game. He loves his work, family, self, and life. Oh, he also has time to use the club that he never had time to visit before. He is even learning to play golf.

How about Steve? Here is his New Story:

I am a master of managing my physical and emotional energy. I approach each day with an eye toward excellence. As I grow I continue to extend my potential. My middle name is "discipline." I live my life in the present. My life is a game that I love to play. I am forgiving of myself for my inability to be perfect. I am fully engaged with whoever is in front of me. I am comfortable with my level of external success. I let go of counterproductive thoughts and feelings.

As Steve got to work on his New Story he began to find that much of his Old Story was just words that he had been repeating that blocked him from seeing other options. Once he got to work on his New Story, by using focus and other coaching sessions in this book, his results kicked in quickly. He dropped 10 pounds within one month. He ritualized turning his phone off by 8 pm nightly to disconnect from work, and spent two hours reading or watching TV before bed. No more last minute checking for emails. He renewed his commitment to a daily workout before going into the office. He started meditating every morning before checking for messages from the office. Each night that he was home before his son went to sleep he would spend time with him, helping him with homework and hearing about his day. He came up with a method for letting go of upsetting thoughts. He carries a journal and any time he is upset he writes it down. At the end of his day, he looks at what is on his page, then tears it out and throws it away to metaphorically let them go. He has made many steps on the journey and is not done yet. He is totally in the game.

Your own New Story is whatever you want it to be. What is the star you want to shoot for? Sit back, meditate. What do you want in your life going forward? Put some of these thoughts, wishes, dreams in a big bucket. There are no rules. Play with it. Put stuff in. Take it out. This is yours and yours alone. It's private. It is for your deepest self. Don't worry about the reasons why not. Use "why yes," it works better. Put it all in the big bucket and let it simmer. Don't get too specific about things: jobs, cars, houses—stuff like that is important, but the stew will taste a lot better when you stick to ways you want to feel and be.

Adam, a successful VP at a large institutional bank said that he wanted more than anything to hit the ball out of the park at work, be an extraordinary father, spouse, and son. His New Story included feeling free of corporate rules so that he could be just as friendly with the mail room employees as the C suite executives.

Scott, out of work after years on Wall Street, his wife recently ill, kids in college, wanted freedom. That is what he imagined, that's what he saw as his New Story's central theme.

Karen, a track superstar, wanted her mental strength to exceed her physical prowess. She wanted to be known as the fiercest competitor, not get sick after races, and live up to her own expectations . . . she wanted this even more than she craved the trophies.

Dean's story was one of being free of his mental darkness and to be valued at the firm where he was employed.

Deidre wanted to feel unburdened from her business, feel free of the need for external validation, find her passion, and embrace all of the parts of herself.

I wanted to experience love in my marriage, pride in my work, and more time with my kids.

A hedge fund executive I once worked with had a 200-million-dollar bank account and he wanted to be willing to take enough risks so that he could have a billion-dollar bank account.

Each of these folks wrote their New Stories and they are so far from their Old Stories now, they are so immersed in the New Stories they are living, if I were to give them their Old Stories again, they would barely recognize them.

You may want to be someone who has the flexibility to travel, to be courageous enough to leave a failing marriage, to be secure enough to lose weight, to be confident enough to learn another language. Maybe you are tired of being a procrastinator, or risk averse, or biting your nails, diving into the potato chips before going to sleep, or maybe you hate always being in a hurry.

It can be something very small or super large. I had a relatively small Old Story about playing the Atlanta Senior Invitational tournament each May: *The players from the southeast have a big advantage because they have been playing outdoors in the heat. I am at a disadvantage because I've mostly played indoors, and I am not used to the heat and humidity.*

Year after year, this Old Story became my destiny for the week. I would play too aggressively on the slow clay court. The heat would always exhaust me, and I would run out of steam. The story I told myself would play out, regardless of my training regimen. In 2009, I consciously changed my story. Carol was going through chemotherapy and demonstrating courage in her battle. She inspired me. My New Story was one of *taking on the challenges, fighting through the difficulties, welcoming the adversity.* I even changed my mental approach to the slower game and the heat. *The slow courts favor my speed and movement on the court. I can choose to play a more patient game. As for the heat and humidity, my muscles feel more flexible in the southern climate. My opponents are used to it, but I feel better than usual.*

That year I had my best showing, advancing to the semis. Although my hip gave out in that last match, leading to hip surgery, I continued the good story, finishing the match with fighting spirit, pushing through the pain, using Carol's courage as a bar that I reached. The power of the story took over. Last year, after several years away from the game due to two hip surgeries, I returned to Atlanta, my final year in the age group, and had two monster wins, losing in the finals to the best clay court player in the world in a close match. Again, the New Story I told myself was *"I have matured as a player in my time away from the game. I have greater perspective on winning and losing after losing Carol and my hip. I am more fit than my opponents because I have been saving my body and rebuilding for two years while they were playing and breaking down."* The power of these stories never ceases to amaze me, and the seed can come from anywhere.

New Story Guidelines

> What do you really want?
> What really matters to you?
> What would you fight to get?
> What would you be willing to do to get it?
> Write your New Story.
> Don't worry about form: use bullet points, create a
>   narrative, write one word, draw a picture.
> See it in your mind.
> And then, if you can, imagine for just one moment what
>   it would be like to have one of the pieces.
> Put yourself in the story for a moment.
> How good does that feel?
> Is it worth taking a step in that direction?

Now, while you are living your life . . . the one that has already changed from the Old Story by being alert to what doesn't work (stories, attitudes, beliefs, reactions, nonreactions), you will find yourself moving a little closer to your New Story. A small step toward autonomy, freedom, mental toughness. Maybe a step closer to higher self-esteem and good health.

As you move toward being who you want to be in the world, you'll find yourself carried by a current. The current is fueled by the fact that you bought the book, signed the contract, wrote your Old Story, wrote your new one. You have just catalyzed the change you want to be. Now that you have "seen" your Old Story and you know your New Story, you can optimize any other self-help tool in the universe, and it will actually work.

To keep this current moving, I am going to give you 33 of the proven and most powerful coaching sessions. Because every day you will be challenged. The voices of the Old Story will be battling for control. You will want to step into the New Story rather than return to the familiarity of doing what you have always done, but in order to do this, you will need tools to create that win. Losing faith? Don't know what to do next? The tools are the glue that keep you on track, the buoyant water that keeps you from hitting bottom as you take the New Story plunge. They are the angels that support you. These 33 private sessions will bridge the gap between your Old Story and your New Story, so you can experience the delicious new freedom of your New Story.

Dive in! What do you have to lose? By the way, you are already winning.

PART II

33 Personal Coaching Sessions for Living Your Best Story

CHAPTER 6

33 Ways to Leave Your Old Story: Using Tools as Your Live-in Coach

The hard must become habit, the habit must become easy, the easy must become beautiful.

—Doug Henning

W hen I first became a tennis teacher, I had very little technical background. I had very little strategic knowledge. All I knew was what I had learned from watching top players on the court, so when the time came for me to give my first lessons I figured I'd better brush up on a few details. The night before I gave my first lesson, I ran to the library and took out the *Sports*

Illustrated Book of Tennis. I figured I should understand how to grip a racket, how to stand, how to swing . . . the basics. Providing that info is what the student was paying for, right?

There was some truth to that.

But I soon found that being a tennis "pro" was different from being a coach. A pro presented relevant information to help a student improve the way they were doing something; for example, making the ball go higher or lower over the net, getting the racket into ready position for a controlled swing, tossing a serve to change the swing. Good stuff. Important stuff. But that kind of change doesn't come smoothly for most people. Skepticism and doubt surface. The student resists the change and slides back to the old way. They make rushed, out-of-control shots. Their serves land outside the box.

Whenever this happened, their initial enthusiasm dropped off and their thoughts turned to the negative. *I can't do this. It is taking too long. Maybe I should just do it the way I was doing it before. This will never work!* Instead of presenting information about what to change, I learned to teach them to keep their head in the game of change. Like I am teaching you now, with this book; your head also needs to be in the game of change!

My work became teaching the process of change. I learned to whisper in their ears so they could live their dream of making positive changes, on and off the court. For more than 35,000 sessions of working with people who said "I can't do this" I learned to show them it *was* possible, and I provided answers for their loss of faith in the process of change. These are your whispers, your taps on the shoulder, your tips, reboots, and jumpstarts. Your private coaching sessions.

Keep working on something until you get it.

Be willing to sacrifice short-term success for long-term goals.
Lose today to win tomorrow.
When we practice enough it is impossible to stay the same.
Put one foot in front of the other.
Know the goal is out there, but keep your mind on the next step.

Never mind spending a thousand dollars an hour on the coach of your dreams. The tool kit I am about to give you is the coach of a lifetime, and it will never leave your side. I've spent over 40 years researching these tools from the very best guides, mentors, coaches, and psychologists in the human potential field. Whole books and sometimes shelves of books have been written about each of these tools. I read books by those who had studied the very best and came up with ideas that these greats must have used: Steven Covey, Mihaly Csikszentmihalyi, Tony Robbins, Les Brown, Norman Vincent Peale, Og Mandino, Jim Loehr, Jim Collins, Tom Rath, Tim Gallwey. I also studied successful people like Muhammad Ali, Oprah, Sylvester Stallone, Mother Teresa, Mahatma Gandhi, Florence Nightingale, John Wooden, Jay Goldman, Nelson Mandela, Billie Jean King, Viktor Frankl, Jack Welch, Joel Greenblatt, Warren Buffett, Björn Borg, Jimmy Connors, Magic Johnson, Jack Nicklaus, Phil Jackson—I liked to learn from anyone who seemed to be at their best in big moments. And from there I knew what people needed to make gigantic changes in their lives. I have distilled them here: the top tools for happiness, health, and riches, collected throughout my life, and pared down for you, so you can feel the dynamite without wading through the words.

Why 33? A normal human spine has 33 vertebrae. This is your spine, your back, your support. Thirty-three is also, according to the Newton scale, the temperature at which water boils, and this signifies your transformation from one state of being to another. In Biblical times, the number 33 was said to represent the meaning of life.

When we are struggling on our path, we find reasons to discount what will work to help us. Welcome all the wonderful tips and ideas that help us through that adversity. My job in this book is to give you the support you need to maintain focus on your New Story, on your goal, on the dream you want to live. When you tell me you can't do it, these tools remind you that you can. You tell me you are frustrated, these tools turn your frustration into gifts. You say I don't get this and these tools teach you to use the word yet. When you are spinning your wheels, tumbling backward down the hill, falling into the same hole again and again, these tools get you back on the path to the dream of your best story.

Which ones work best? You decide. Thousands of people, both on and off the court, have used one or all of these to keep living New Stories. This is your banquet, choose what feeds your New Story. Some of these sessions will feel similar. You may find one way is more helpful than another. The brain often needs more than one way of seeing a challenge in order to recondition itself. That is what you are doing here, you are reconditioning your brain to move out of the Old Story into the New Story. The sessions are simple and fast; they will boost your morale, your mental toughness, and your ability to have faith in your New Story. It's important to remember these are not dictates, rules or musts. If one coaching session doesn't resonate, move on to the next. Make sure you don't stop moving through the book because you aren't hip with one of the coaching sessions.

Sometimes resistance arises when you engage in a coaching session. Resistance is covered in the "but" section at the end of each chapter. The buts address any smaller fears that might come up. But if you are having a big "but" about the session, remember to either give yourself the opportunity to find a New Story about the element discussed in the coaching session, or simply read on. Just don't stop moving into your New Story. With this coaching, you can tackle anything. Pieces will fall into place and you will be moving in the direction of your dreams. I am here for you as your coach, countering your occasional doubts. So: it's time. Time to not only live your New Story, but continue to live it, day after day!

CHAPTER 7

Blind Faith

Faith is to believe what you do not yet see.
The reward of this faith is to see what you
believe.

—St. Augustine

Faith cannot be contradicted; it is
intuitive conviction of truth, and it cannot
be shaken even by contrary evidence.

—Samuel Johnson

Faith is taking the first step even when
you can't see the whole staircase.

—Martin Luther King, Jr.

In 2011 a former Navy Air rescue swimmer, Brian Dickinson, climbed Mt. Everest, alone, after the Sherpa he'd hired became ill and had to turn back. When the sun rose the next morning, it burned right through his corneas, leaving him not only alone, but blind at 29,035 feet.

Blind, exhausted, and without a guide, he had to cross what is known as the Cornice Traverse, a two mile drop into Tibet or Nepal, depending on which way he fell and, at one point, his oxygen bottle ran out. "Instead of panicking," he told a reporter for the *Sno Valley Star*, "I started moving. Just one step in front of the other . . ." He didn't contemplate the danger, over-analyze, or consider that he may be experiencing the last hours of his life. He just put doubt aside and kept moving. Today Brian Dickinson has regained his sight and is still climbing mountains with his family. In his book *Blind Descent,* he describes the journey and his faith in God that kept him moving down the mountain. Whether our faith is in God, in ourselves, in a process, or in a person, faith is one of the most powerful tools we have toward living a New Story.

Too much skepticism and you sabotage your New Story. Skepticism keeps you from taking action. Skepticism, the word, originated in Plato's Academy around 270 BCE. when a guy named Pyrrho was so skeptical of the dangers his friends warned him about, he was always getting rescued from the paths of speeding carts and the edges of cliffs. Faith does not mean waiting for something to happen to see if it actually will, it means moving forward when the results have not shown up yet.

Neil Strauss, a *New York Times* and *Rolling Stone* reporter, who wrote *The Truth,* a book on addiction, relates a conversation he had with a mentor about getting clean, whereby the mentor tells him he'll never find sobriety until he puts skepticism aside and plunges in. This is, at first, abhorrent to Neil, who has been intellectualizing advice from practitioners and counselors in order to stay in his Old Story. But it's often only in putting skepticism away and having blind faith that we experience monumental shifts in our lives as Neil eventually did. Blind faith in a process, in our abilities, in the realization of a dream, can be the secret sauce that allows us to take action in the direction we want to go.

This is particularly true when you are moving toward your New Story. The easy path is doubt. Doubt keeps us in our Old Story, *I've never changed before, why will this be any different? I'm not a success story, my whole family is middle-of-the-road and I am, too. I'm not a risk taker, a networker, a people person, a ladies man.* But the world is full of people who put skepticism aside and lived a New Story.

Clint Eastwood transitioned from being a spaghetti western actor to being a top director.

Jack Johnson went from being a janitor to being a music star.

Marie Curie went from struggling through poverty to get a good education, to discovering radium and inventing the mobile x-ray machine and being the first woman to receive two Nobel prizes. Somewhere all of them had to put skepticism aside and take action.

How do you court blind faith? You simply notice doubt as a judge that wants to keep you in your Old Story and answer it with faith in the New Story. You acknowledge that there are forces at work you cannot see that could be helping you, showing you a new way, giving you hope.

Many years ago, when my wife, Carol, was still alive, she went for a psychic reading. Part of the reading was about past lives, and the psychic told her that in a past life she was a hummingbird. This was so similar to Carol's personality, she buzzed around, never stopping, she had incredible energy and would move from person to person, drawing out their sweetness and then giving it to the next person.

We were in Barnes & Noble several years later, and I saw a coffee table book on hummingbirds. I bought it for Carol and several days later, she opened the book and burst into tears when she saw the inside cover . . . there was a sketch of a cave wall with hieroglyphics and pictures of hummingbirds. To me this meant that she had some long deep connection. She just laughed it off, perhaps with a bit of skepticism.

Nearly twenty years passed with never another thought about hummingbirds until two weeks after she died. I was at my cousin's house in Montauk, sitting on the deck early in the morning, alone. All of a sudden there was a hummingbird buzzing around the flowers. I had never seen one, just pictures. I asked my cousin if she had many hummingbirds around and she said, no, never.

I called my daughter Jody to tell her, and she, shocked, said that she too had never seen one, and yet when she was leaving a store in New Jersey the day before, she saw one herself. Later I talked to Rita, Carol's cousin, who remembered the story of Carol crying from the book and said that she had gone to visit her daughter in Staten Island. While sitting on a stoop, as she and Carol used to do when growing up in Brooklyn, she saw, for the first time in her life, a hummingbird, which stayed around her for a long time.

A few weeks later I was in Aspen, walking with my three-year-old granddaughter Madelyn. She was staring at and pointing at a huge planter of flowers. She was showing me a tiny tiny hummingbird. A local stopped and told us we must be very special because that was a hummingbird moth and they rarely came out in the middle of the day

These stories go on and on, and it is always Carol's presence when the hummingbirds arrive. How does this happen? Who knows? When we have faith that strange things can happen, we are open to the miracle of looking at a nocturnal hummingbird in the middle of the day with our granddaughter. You may be buoyed by unseen forces. I am not being bizarre here. I am just encouraging you to relax in the notion that you can't know everything, so you might as well have faith. When we have faith, we can admit that, yes, maybe change really can happen, everything might fall into alignment, the dream you have been wishing for can come true. You may not know the full story yet, but you can have faith in your own ability, your own dream, in the people around you, in the instinctive response that chose this path.

Still in doubt? Answer that skepticism with action. Show the doubter that you mean business. This may take the form of reading a different coaching session: visualization, rereading your New Story, asking the can question (more on this in Chapter 19); or it may take the form of a phone call, sending an email. It may mean turning the next page in a book, allowing yourself to suspend doubt for one more minute so you can defy the voice of the skeptic inside and rely on the inexorable power of blind faith to see you through, as Brian Dickinson did, when he blindly made it down one of the biggest mountains in the world.

SESSION TIP

The Big But: But I'm afraid that if I believe in something with blind faith, I will wind up disappointed, like diving into a pool, and really there isn't any water in it.

Try This On for Size: Remember that disappointment is only temporary, but staying the same lasts a lifetime. In fact disappointment can be a portal, leading you to the next thing. Oh! I didn't win this, but I got asked to do another; Oh! I didn't get that job, but I honed my interviewing skills. And because having Blind Faith feels so good at the time (who doesn't want to believe everything will turn out like we want it to?) it often yields incredible results. The chapter Redefine Winning (Chapter 17) can help tremendously with believing in the power of Blind Faith and helping us see the true golden lining in almost anything.

CHAPTER 8

Role-Playing the New Story

> The golden opportunity you are seeking is
> in yourself. It is not in your environment,
> it is not in luck or chance, or the help of
> others; it is in yourself alone.
>
> —ORISON SWETT MARDEN

Katy walked into my office in March of her senior year of high school. She had just competed in an exclusive field in the Millrose Game mile for top high school milers at Madison Square Garden. And she had come in dead last. Not just last but way behind the rest of the field. She was already one of the elite in the country to have gained entry into this race, but she was still highly discouraged.

As we talked, she presented her Old Story:

I get anxious on days of races. These feelings escalate as the race gets closer. I often hope the race will be cancelled. I'm afraid that when the pain comes I won't be able to hold my pace, and I race in fear a lot, feeling I am not as good as my competitors. I had really great results when I first started, but I struggle to pull it together like I used to.

"It's amazing you still run great times," I said to Katy. "When you consider how many mental ankle weights you are carrying."

The ankle weights were stories she had come to believe were true. And, in some ways they were true. No matter how accomplished Katy was, the stories had created a gap between who she currently was as a runner and who she aspired to be.

One week later this was Katy's New Story:

I get excited and eager on days leading up to my races. These feelings escalate as I get closer to the race. All my races are opportunities to improve. I handle pain like a champion. When the pain comes I challenge myself to conquer this beast. I fear no competitor. I deserve to be racing at a high level. I am just as good as everyone who tows the line. My past successes drive me.

"But that story is not who I am," Katy told me.

Of course not," I told her. "That's the story of where you will *go*."

"But how can I close the gap between feeling anxious and feeling excited?"

So I asked her a question that you can ask yourself whenever you are trying to get out of a place of extreme stress: "If you were already living your New Story, what would you be doing before races?"

Immediately, Katy answered, "I would do deep breathing. I would stretch. I would tell myself that all races are opportunities for me to improve, win or not."

Yes. She was role-playing her New Story self.

Once she knew how she would be acting if she was already living her New Story, she was able to start changing the way she acted. Before races she would notice if she was telling her Old Story. She realized it was story and she could take a step, even a small one toward the New Katy Story. She started breathing and stretching in these moments. She did it to run better and to improve at the skill of storytelling. Two for one, closing the gap between who she had been and who she would become while winning more races.

While this sort of change won't always happen overnight, there's no rule about change saying it's impossible. (See the Data Shmata coaching session in Chapter 21) Two months later, in the National Scholastic mile (her final high school race), she won. National champion. The #1 high school miler in the USA. Less than one year later she won the silver medal in the Junior World Championships and has gone on to help Villanova University continue to be a powerhouse in Women's' Division 1 Track. Katy keeps writing new stories about who she needs to be to get a shot at the upcoming Olympics, and she closes the gap by asking herself who her New Story self would be during races.

Is she done?

We are never fully done with closing the gap, and that's what's so incredibly freeing about it. Wherever you are feeling anxious, uncomfortable, unfulfilled, unhappy; whenever you can see the gap between who you are today and who you want to be, let your mind take a leap. Read your New Story and ask yourself: If I were that person, what tools would I use to approach this challenge?

Katy may make the Olympics; she may not. But she has an edge over many other athletes: she has story writing, and in every facet of her life she can use it to close the gap between who she is, and who she aspires to be.

Another one of my clients was overly worried about her weight, her health, her job, and her relationship. She was 50 pounds overweight, in a dead-end relationship with a married man, and working long hours at a job she hated. "What would you feel if you were living your New Story?" I asked her. "I'd feel so grateful!" was the first thing she said. So I asked her to promise to email me gratitudes every day. Sometimes her grats were small. She had a beautiful view of the park, her neighbor walked her dog when she was delayed, the barista at her coffee shop remembered her name. Other days she would write big ones: that she was grateful for her health or that she had incredible friends and family. Sometimes she wrote more than 60 grats a day. After a year and a half, she had lost 50 pounds, gotten out of the relationship with the married guy, and had quit her job and started a successful coaching business. Today she's living the New Story she had role-played 18 months earlier.

The New Story is you, it's just you in the future. Leaping time to become the New Story will help you act in a way that will train you to believe you are already living the New Story, until, probably faster than you think, the external world will align to match that role-play. It's a miraculous tool, and one that takes only a second to try. Have fun with it!

What do you have to lose?

SESSION TIP

The Big But: But when I role-play, I feel slightly ridiculous, like I'm lying to myself and not really being authentic.

Try This On For Size: Yes! The point of role-playing is to feel out of our skin and uncomfortable. The more you playact at a feeling, the more you begin to get comfortable with it, until the mind can't feel the difference between the authentic feeling and the role-played one. That's when they begin to merge. If you aren't uncomfortable, you aren't doing it right!

CHAPTER 9

The Mini-Story: Creating Achievable Milestones

If you can't fly, then run, if you can't run, then walk, if you can't walk, then crawl, but whatever you do, you have to keep moving forward.

—MARTIN LUTHER KING, JR.

A few years ago, I was working with a chiropractor named Bill. He's a guy whose heart is in the right place but he had gotten into trouble with the law. Insurance fraud. He was fortunate that despite being convicted a judge vacated his sentence, including fines and a three-month prison term. His reputation was ruined and he was finished as a chiropractor.

He had to work hard to gain trust of his friends and to feel like he still belonged in his community. He was looked at as a liar and a cheat and, he admitted, he was. But he wanted a second chance. A chance to redeem himself in the eyes of those around him.

He came up with a big New Story. *I am devoted, full time, to making the lives of others better.* He devoted his life to philanthropic causes. He's been recognized for his work for the youth enrichment programs he runs for kids who are at risk and has been given multiple awards for his work as an inspiration to kids who are from needy communities. He created a foundation that raises money to provide college educations for the underprivileged. He is loved by the kids and is viewed by his community as someone who really turned it around and is truly giving back.

But he still had an empty feeling inside. Despite doing things that looked meaningful to the outside world, when we talked he began to unload a lot of troublesome, Old Story stuff. *Even though I look like I'm succeeding, I'm really not doing as well as I could be. I'm making a difference, but there's an incomplete emptiness in my life. This feeling of being incomplete isn't concrete, but there's a gnawing sensation that something is missing.*

Bill had been down so far that he felt that he needed a huge New Story. A story that, although he seemed to reach it, was missing personal meaning. He had satisfied all of those around him but had missed the smaller steps that might have made him feel more complete. While reaching for the stars he had neglected some smaller important pieces of his life. The pieces that might have built a better foundation for his new external successes. Slowing down. Spending meaningful time with his own kids. Sure they were at the awards dinners but ironically he didn't have time to throw a ball around with them. He gained weight because he was too busy taking care of the big story to be good to himself. His friends, who had been so important to him in his earlier life, had been ignored for the money people who would contribute to his causes. His New Story was too big. So we worked on some smaller, mini stories that would fulfill him in other ways: *I slow down to smell the roses. I am fully engaged with my kids. I do what is best for my body each day. I make time to spend meaningful moments with my friends.*

By reading his mini stories and taking steps in their direction he has found a new level of satisfaction in his life and his big story continues to evolve. He makes a difference in the lives of those close to him and of those who hardly even know him.

There are the big stories of our lives, coaches talk of the "ultimate life mission": health, work, family, faith, community. But sometimes the big story feels so overwhelming, it's hard to know where to start. Don't get yourself hung up on a story that may take a lifetime to achieve. That is okay. There's no need to over-reach on the stories. Break the big ones down to mini-stories. Life gives us myriad opportunities to break the big ones down to mini-stories. In time, they can take you to the biggest stories.

Write one about how you handle your phone. *My smartphone goes mute the moment I enter my home.* Write one about how you manage your stress. *I take one mini-break a day to cleanse my mind.* Those are small stories that can make you feel you are moving forward.

One of my client's, Vicki, was in the midst of a storm at work. Her jewelry business was taking off like wildfire, her husband was working 17 hours a day, she was having difficulty getting her team to work together, she was using her apartment to show her merchandise, and she was struggling to find the time to design her products. She was totally overwhelmed and was starting her days frazzled and ineffectively. She created mini-stories about what she did to start her day that led to her being the way she had declared in her New Story: *I am calm. I am focused. I walk slowly through the day, breathing deeply.* She found focus by washing the dishes. She found calm by observing five breaths. Just a couple of mini-stories.

Mini-stories are most important when we feel overwhelmed by all that we would like to improve in our lives. When the concepts are too huge for the mind to contemplate. When Old Stories contain huge concepts—peace at any price, owning success means hurting others, everyone in the business world is like the crooks I worked with, I'm so hurt I can't even contemplate another relationship—you can still read your New Story over every day, and you can work toward it, but sometimes having some mini-stories is the best way to move toward living that New Story.

Health? How is this for a mini story? *I choose a healthy snack during my three o'clock break. Rather than send an email to an office mate, I walk over and ask him in person. I take the stairs instead of the elevator. My smartphone goes mute on Sundays.* When you are feeling stuck on the path to the big stories, write a mini. It is important that we really get our stories straight so that we can move toward our destinies. And mini-stories are specific, they are clear, they aren't difficult to accomplish, they show us that it doesn't have to be difficult to get to where we want to go.

SESSION TIP

The Big But: But when I'm working on an achievable milestone it feels too small, I need to be working on something bigger.

Try This On For Size: In fact when we practice with small stories, we become experts with bigger stories—organically. Kaizen (Chapter 13) helps you see how multimillion dollar companies made gigantic inroads by taking small steps.

CHAPTER 10

Your Secret Power

I just saw this shot doing a crazy thing,
but even though it was crazy, I knew it
was the only way to get the ball near
the hole.

—BUBBA WATSON, GOLF CHAMPION

In Genevieve Behrand's book, *Your Invisible Power,* perhaps the first text to openly talk about the power of visualization, she points out that everyone visualizes, whether they know it or not. And directed visualizing is the great secret of success. She talks about needing $20,000 to go study with her mentor in Europe. She had no idea how she was going to get it, but every night, she envisioned counting out the bills while feeling very confident that it was actually happening.

We now fly through the air, not because anyone has been able to change the laws of nature, but because, when things were challenging, one Wright brother would say to the other, "It's all right, brother, I can see myself riding in that machine, and it travels easily and steadily." Those Wright Brothers knew what they wanted, and kept their pictures constantly before them.

The popular shtick is about visualizing big things, a trip, a new house, flying a plane, winning the lottery. But what about if you want to change a behavior?

One of my favorite clients is a doctor named Jeff. He is the senior oncologist in a major group in New York City. This guy is about as capable as one can be: amazing focus, endurance, attitude, and skill. Totally together. Except for one thing, when his dad, a big time surgeon, is critical of him, he can't handle it. He turns to jelly. He feels like a little kid. He wanted to tell his dad that he was soon to get engaged to a woman who wasn't the same religion as his family, and he knew it was going to be met with disapproval. His Old Story was holding him back: *I am a cowardly lion. Other people's opinions make me melt.* His New Story: *I speak my truth fearlessly. I am nonreactive to what others say about me.* Your secret power, visualization to the rescue. He used it as a dress rehearsal. He kept seeing the meeting in his mind. Seeing his story play out. A few times a day, he'd visualize walking into his dad's home, sitting in the chair he would likely sit in. He'd take a deep breath. Calm. Certain. Fearless. Speaking the truth, being nonreactive to the response, saying the words he had visualized. "Thank you, Dad, for your input." He could see it when he practiced. He did it several times a day, each time feeling more familiar with it. Nothing fancy. Just straightforward.

When the time came, he had lived it in his mind enough that he was able to speak his truth. His father acted exactly as he thought he would. But Jeff didn't turn into a child again; he stayed happy and grounded about his engagement. That is the power of visualization. He couldn't change his dad, but he realized he didn't need to, he only needed to change himself.

Visualization turned out to be his greatest tool for success. He'd been very anxious about public speaking and felt terrible at it. Yet he was often asked to present at conferences. But after that first success with visualizing his talk with this father, he began visualizing daily that he was an extraordinary speaker. He speaks in front of major audiences at some of the most important conferences in the world. When called on, he is used as an expert on the morning shows. That's a long way from melting in front of his dad.

Jim Carrey used it to snag $10 million for his role in *Dumb and Dumber*, Kerri Walsh and Misty May-Treanor, the dynamic volleyball duo have used it to win three gold medals, and Oprah Winfrey used it to become one of the most powerful entertainment personalities in the world.

When I started making some progress in my tennis and competing with the best in my age group, I had an inkling of a dream: that I could someday win a national championship. As a ten-year-old I used to lie in bed and see the end of a game in my mind, I was making the last shot to win it. Without knowing it, I was visualizing.

As an adult, I became that little boy again, picturing myself, over and over, hitting a winner at a National on the final point. And then I would see both my arms go up and a slow walk to the net for a handshake. The first time I won a National, someone took a picture of me right when I won, my arms were up, just as I had seen it so many times, exactly the same pose. I have a picture frame with me in that pose after each national championship I have won. The visualization became my signature.

Science shows us we stimulate the same brain regions when we visualize an action, as when we actually perform that same action. For example, if you imagine yourself hitting a baseball every night, when you get back to home plate, you will perform as well as someone who actually did hit a baseball every night. This works best in pictures. For the brain, a picture's worth a thousand words. See your New Story happening, visualize yourself behaving in the way that you want to act, and allow the astonishing power of your imagination to do the work.

SESSION TIP

The Big But: I can picture it so clearly, but I am frustrated because I am not there yet.

Try This On For Size: That frustration is part of the fuel that will enable you to make change. When we see the gap between where we are and where we know we are going, the mind instantly begins to close that gap. That frustration you're struggling against? It is part of the impetus for this closing. Anytime the mind is uncomfortable, it is automatically going to find ways to feel comfortable.

Don't stop visualizing; the more you visualize, the more your mind will find ways to make the dream happen.

CHAPTER 11

Dancing with the Beast

We must embrace pain and burn it as fuel
for our journey.

—KENJI MIYAZAWA

A problem is a chance for you to do your
best.

—DUKE ELLINGTON

For the last ten years I've been coaching at one of the biggest, most consistently successful hedge funds on Wall Street. Most of the people who work there are between 25 and 45 years old and in a stretch of their lives where succeeding at their game, picking stocks, is at the top of their to-do list. Every day their battle is to make the most educated picks based on public information, past history of how stocks react to news, and an ability to read the mood of an irrational market.

Their scorecard is money. You make it. You are a winner. You don't make it? You're a failure. When they make money, they get lots of material stuff that creates cultural envy like beautiful homes in the suburbs, nice cars, club memberships and dinners at the best restaurants, and financial security for their families.

But as much security as many have, they are often unhappy because their scorecard is not as big as their buddy's or not as big as it could have been if they had invested a bigger amount, bought sooner, or sold later. If they lose, it feels like food is being taken off their table. And many complain. *I am frustrated. This is my worst trading day ever. Things are so tough in my sector. My boss is not letting me buy a position that I know will make money. The market is crazy. The news from Greece and China is making it impossible for me to do my job.*

And I tell them, "These are the beasts of this game, these are the beasts of your chosen job. All jobs have beasts. If you don't like the ones in yours, there's a guy on the corner of 55th Street and Fifth Ave, selling hats and scarves. But he has a beast too. For him it is the weather." They have all heard about Katy, the runner. Her beast was pain and, at age 19, she found a way to make the pain her running partner. We have to be comfortable with the beasts that are part of what we do.

One of the biggest beasts of their work is that they can lose huge amounts of money in a moment and they have to try to stay even, which is hard to do when the stakes are high. The trick? Don't resist the beast. Make the beast your friend. Love the beast. Include the beast in your New Story.

If you think this is impossible, take a quick look at his Holiness, the 14th Dalai Lama. He started his life on a straw mat in a cowshed in the middle of nowhere in Tibet, and has had to endure Chinese occupation where thousands of years of culture and religion were attacked, and finally suffered exile to India, and yet he has become the most popular world leader. Why? Because he saw these beasts as opportunities to grow stronger rather than to be victimized. "Whenever there is a challenge," he has said. "There is also an opportunity to face it, to demonstrate and develop our will and determination." We put the beasts on a leash and walk with them rather than getting in the ring with them.

Once a week, I teach tennis to one of my hedge fund clients on the court at his house. His Old Story was that he had AADD (adult attention deficit disorder), and he told me he couldn't focus on the court because of it. This is partly true; he's always jumping from one thing to the other. "Why did I miss that shot?" he might ask, and before I can answer: "Do you think that tree over there is dying or just hasn't blossomed yet?"

But a beast like AADD can also show up as an excuse not to win, not to reach that goal, not to get what you really want. So I made the beast his friend. I told him AADD was the perfect mindset for tennis where the points last less than ten seconds. And as an equities trader? Another perfect addition to his recipe for success. A business where you are supposed to be a master of leaving the last moment and being in the next.

Every activity comes with "beasts." Some jobs come with financial ups and downs. Others have the beast of bad weather. Speaking the truth in a relationship has the beast of being misunderstood or hurtful to another. Hell, even a day at the beach includes walking on hot sand and lugging chairs and umbrellas. Baseball has errors. Football has fumbles. Doctors face the risk of lawsuits. How does your beast make you stronger? How does it actually work for you? Why does it give you an edge? Welcome them. They are, after all, part of the way things are, and once you move the beast from being a good excuse to a fortifying friend, it frees you up to get the best out of what you are doing.

SESSION TIP

The Big But: But I'm afraid that if I keep this up, dancing with all this stuff that feels like a burden, I will start to burn out and get too tired to move on.

Try This On For Size: The beast of burnout is the one that threatens everything you are working hard for. When you feel you are heading toward burnout, nap time (Chapter 26) is one of the best answers. If rest isn't possible, remember that if you are worried about burnout, you are usually future tripping. Stay in the present and Focus (Chapter 16) on the next step (Kaizen, Chapter 13).

CHAPTER 12

Changing Your Ringtone

What you focus on expands, and when
you focus on the goodness in your life,
you create more of it. Opportunities,
relationships, even money flowed my way
when I learned to be grateful, no matter
what happened in my life.

—OPRAH WINFREY

Writing gratitudes has become pretty popular these days. Around the stock market crash of 2008, Shawn Achor, the Harvard University positive psychology professor, wrote about the benefits of writing them. But during tough times, it's difficult to remember to be grateful. We often think we don't have time for it, or we are afraid there's nothing there.

The ringtone for my phone was never that important to me.

I just picked a song that I liked, something with a good beat by the Black Eyed Peas. Sometime during the three years that Carol was fighting cancer, my phone went on the fritz and my ringtone disappeared. Without giving it much thought I used a song that I heard on someone else's phone at work one day. It was a nice song, had a good beat, and John Mayer was a new voice I liked. I didn't think too much about the words. But it must have drawn me because of the message. It must have seeded in my consciousness because after Carol lost her battle, someone mentioned how, "Waiting for the World to Change" seemed fitting for me.

I had no idea that every day, every time I got a call, I was reinforcing the message that I was waiting for the world to change. During the early days after her death, it was challenging to feel grateful for what I had. I was reinforcing an Old Story. That ringtone kept reminding me that I was waiting to feel grateful.

One day, many months later, I was feeling lighter, I had recovered from surgery. I had met Jo Ann, another grandchild was on the way, my clients were growing in number, my tennis was improving. I was driving to my sister's house to have lunch and I was singing along with a song on the radio. *Blue skies, shining on me, nothing but blue skies . . . all I see.* Willie Nelson and I doing a duet. I didn't think about how the words were reminding me of how grateful I had been feeling in my life, despite my loss. But that night, I decided it was time to let go of "Waiting on the World to Change." It was time to make "Blue Skies" my new ringtone.

Every call that I got was a reminder of being grateful for what I had. I was no longer waiting for the world to change. It was up to me. When at work in an office, everybody gets a good jolt when my phone rings. Sometimes when I walk in they play it. Bob's theme song.

Writing gratitudes is a way to shift from your Old Story to your New Story. Why? Because during those inevitable times that it feels things are going against you, you are vulnerable to slipping right back into your Old Story. It's invaluable to have a bag of appreciation for all that you have. If you have your health, that's a big one. And the health of those around you is another big one. A roof over your head is invaluable, food to eat, water you can safely drink, the ability to see when you open your eyes in the morning, being able to read, having a job, friends, family, money to put food on the table. And the small ones: remembering to bring an umbrella on a rainy day, nice weather, a smile from a stranger, clean sheets on your bed, the laughter of a child, a phone call from a friend. If you can carry this bag of gratitudes with you all the time, when you hit some rough patches, it will help you remember that life is good.

After Carol died, I would get up each morning, sit at the kitchen table, and write. I'd start with just three gratitudes and before I knew it, the list went on and on. It never seemed to matter if they were big grats: *I am healthy, I have a home, I can drink water out of the tap without fear of illness, this morning I woke up.* They could be small: *I remembered to buy berries for my granola* or *I got a good parking space at the train station.* Grats helped me stay away from the victim mentality and shifted the way I saw the world. Sure there was a bad thing going on, I'd lost the love of my life to cancer. But no matter how big that was, there were always things to be grateful for. Blue skies.

That's when I began to challenge the guys in the firm to write them every day to see if they could maintain a more positive attitude in their world of worry and fear. Seven years later many in the firm are still writing them. Despite losing money on a trade, as they do, about 45 percent of the time, they feel grateful for what they have, their thinking has shifted monumentally.

Recently, Alan, one of the most successful, emailed me when he was in a bad streak. "Do you want to be frustrated?" I asked him. "Does it help your profit and loss statement to be frustrated? If you want to shift how you feel," I told him, "without having to immediately change your PNL, I have a great exercise for you: write your gratitudes."

He sighed. "But that's hard."

"Really?" I asked him. "How hard is it? Does it take as much courage as investing $1 million in one position? Just write them and you will be moving forward toward your story of being an extraordinary investor." He did and, at least for that day, his life began to shift.

Robert Emmons, Ph.D., a University of California, Davis, professor, did eight years of intensive research on gratitude in his best-selling book, *Thanks! How the New Science of Gratitude Can Make You Happier.* Some of his findings are amazing, lower blood pressure, improved immune function, and better sleep. Gratitude reduces the risk of depression, anxiety, and substance abuse disorders. It helps prevent suicide, lowers your cholesterol and blood pressure, and helps people eat better, exercise more, and take better care of their health.

What's really exciting is that gratitude is iterative. When you notice things you are grateful for, you activate a part of your brain called the reticular activating system. Your RAS is similar to a filter between your conscious and your subconscious mind. So, if your intention is to buy a blue Volvo, you may start seeing blue Volvos everywhere. When you write gratitudes, you begin to see things to be grateful for everywhere. You don't have to write them, you can think them, say them, or simply notice what you are grateful for. Brain science shows that what you focus on grows. Most of all, be grateful for ways you are moving toward your New Story, even the small steps you take, and you will begin to be more grateful every day.

SESSION TIP

The Big But: But if I only focus on the positive and not the negative, the negative will just keep kicking my you-know-what!

Try This On For Size: Gratitudes aren't either/or. In fact, when we think about what we are grateful for, we give the mind a break, and in that break comes the ability to make choices about what isn't going so well. Remember that writing your Old Story is a form of focusing on what isn't working, so that you can change it. Gratitudes allow us the strength to make that change.

CHAPTER 13

Kaizen:
One Step, One Step

Grain by grain, a loaf of bread; stone by
stone, a castle.

—Yugoslavian proverb

When nothing seems to help, I go and look
at a stonecutter hammering away at his
rock, perhaps a hundred times without as
much as a crack showing in it. Yet at the
hundred and first blow it will split in two,
and I know it was not that last blow that
did it, but all that had gone before.

—Jacob A. Riis

n 1986, the Japanese businessman Masaaki Imai wrote a book
called *"Kaizen: The Key to Japan's Competitive Success."* Today
many organizations use *kaizen* as a long-term competitive
strategy. There's a lot to *kaizen*. It emphasizes the well-being

of the employee; working smarter, not harder; and developing best practices so that workers don't have to think. But one of *Kaizen's* strongest aspects is this idea of incremental, ongoing improvement.

We tend not to use *kaizen* in this country, and that might be why the self-help industry is so gigantic and people fail so often. The books are demanding huge change, they often aren't about small iterative steps. Not honoring *kaizen* is probably the reason so many businesses fail, too. We tend to think small steps don't amount to anything. Take the auto industry. When it became apparent that engines broke down frequently because of the heat generated by the materials, the industry realized they needed to move toward ceramic parts. Detroit stormed ahead, going great guns, building ceramic engines without bothering to first gain a solid understanding of how to use these materials. The engines broke down causing a huge economic crisis. In Japan, they approached this work using *kaizen,* they began to buy ceramics companies and invested in the slow incremental growth of learning how to work with ceramics. Their engines became basically trouble free.

As you continue becoming your New Story, it can be a gift to understand that it really happens just one step at a time, any movement away from the old and toward the new puts us in a different place, with a different view. The old moves into the rearview mirror and the New Story, which once seemed so far away is just a little closer. If, each day, you take one step, although you may not notice it, you will have traveled quite far. "It's like driving at night with the headlights on," E. L. Doctorow has said. "You can only see a little ways ahead of you, but you can make the whole journey that way." E. L. Doctorow has written a dozen of the most celebrated novels in American literary history. He did it using *kaizen*.

Back when I was recovering from hip surgery and needed to walk every day, I decided to go to a community that had a lot of rolling hills so I could build up muscle. One day, I was half way through my walk and facing a hill that just looked too hard. It was steep and long, and I felt fatigued before I'd even taken the first step. Then I remembered: a journey of a thousand miles begins with one step. So I took that step. I knew I could take one step again. And again. I kept taking steps without being concerned about how many and how far I still had to go. Before I knew it, I was at the top of the hill. I felt like Rocky when he reaches the top of the stone steps at the Philadelphia Museum of Art. The truth is, we are almost never too tired to take one step.

Knowing that you only need the strength to take one step can be very calming. My client Stacy was unhappy in her career, and I was coaching her through the lucrative sale of her business. But the day after she sold it, she woke up and started freaking out. *What have I done?* She feared she wouldn't know how to spend her days, she wouldn't have enough money to travel and go out for dinner, attend the theater. She got scared that she no longer had group health insurance. Money, identity, security, these are huge factors to consider. They are too huge. She needed to take a step back from the macro picture and take a shot at the micro. Just look at one step. She spoke to her accountant one day, studied insurance policies another day. Another day she joined a women's group. Instead of trying to live a brand new life immediately, she took one step at a time toward her New Story, the best story of her life.

Goliath's steps are too big. They're impressive but not practical. Change happens less when we make huge commitments: I'm going to join the gym and work out six times a week and more when we simply notice that we want the piece of cake before we go to bed. That's your first step, noticing. You haven't stepped on a treadmill yet. The next night, you might notice that desire again and just have a cookie. The next night, when the need for something sweet arises, maybe you'll reach for a piece of fruit. This will progress, until one day you will step on the treadmill, and it will seem like no big deal.

Big change can be scary to the mind that craves stasis. I have a great client, Mike, who really does the work. He's amazing, and he's probably moving the most out of all my clients. During one of talks, he started kicking around the idea of leaving finance and starting a new business. He got excited about creating his own environment, having control over his life. But after that phone call, he started getting nervous. The next time we talked he told me he'd gotten so nervous about our last conversation that he started to want to back off from me. He was scared he was going down a frightening path, and he just needed to slow down a bit. The change was too huge. He opted for *kaizen*. Talking about it is not the same as leaving a career and staring a new one.

Lots of stuff comes up when we start to shine the light on the Old Story and move toward the New Story. Taking small baby steps can help with that. The trick with kaizen is to celebrate the small steps. Today I ate the cake, but I noticed it. That's one step. Simply buying this book is a step.

I tell most of the people I work with that their homework is to start with five deep breaths in the morning. Many of them are used to dealing with millions of dollars every day and they aren't used to small. "Five breaths?" they ask me incredulously. "Yeah," I say. "Get up, eat breakfast, brush your teeth, check the news, whatever, and then sit in your living room and just notice yourself taking five breaths." Once that small awareness is cultivated, it's easier to go on to another step. This first small step of building the self-discipline muscle can lead to quitting drinking, better relationships, more money, and a host of other gigantic changes.

Never lose an opportunity of urging a practical beginning, however small," Florence Nightingale once said. "For it is wonderful how often in such matters the mustard-seed germinates and roots itself." During the Crimean War, Nightingale and her nurses transformed the British hospital where they were working. In six months, the death rate of patients fell from 40 percent to 2 percent. She wrote about 200 books, pamphlets, and reports on hospital, sanitation, and other health-related issues and transformed hospital care worldwide. She did it using *kaizen*.

The mind seems to be afraid of change. If I told you that tomorrow you had to quit any habit you have—no matter how dangerous to yourself or others—cold turkey—you'd balk. But if I told you, take five breaths or walk up the stairs instead of taking the elevator or say hello to your barista at Starbucks in the morning, your mind would probably relax. If it's very afraid of even small change, it might ask you, "What's the use?" But look at the pyramids of Egypt. How were they built? One man raised his dolerite pounder and made the first strike to pulverize the stone that needed to be extracted. And then a second blow was struck. And a third. And eventually the Pyramid of Giza was built. Now, maybe, the steps toward that New Story don't feel so massive. Just one small step, pick your step, any step will do.

SESSION TIP

The Big But: But I'm never going to get up the staircase, I might as well give up, it's too long.

Try This On For Size: Answer your but with a question. Ask yourself what it is that you are ultimately moving toward. Now ask this question: What do I stand to lose by not taking this step?

CHAPTER 14

The Big O

There is nothing either good or bad, but
thinking makes it so.

—WILLIAM SHAKESPEARE

Our life is the creation of our mind.

—BUDDHA

It is better to light the candle than to
curse the darkness.

—ELEANOR ROOSEVELT

Sixty-two years ago, Norman Vincent Peale wrote a book on
optimism called *The Power of Positive Thinking*. The book
was earth shattering. In 1985 two psychologists named Michael
Sheier and Charles Carver did more groundbreaking research
on the power of optimism in a study in *Health Psychology*
that linked psychology to biology: "Optimism, Coping, and
Health: Assessment and Implications of Generalized Outcome

Expectancies." By looking at motivation and goal setting, they realized that if people felt like they were going to succeed, more often than not, they did. And negative thoughts had the reverse affect, if we think we are going to fail, we do. "I'm going to double fault," a tennis player might tell himself. And the body automatically begins to try to support that belief. "My boss, the thinker, is telling me I should double fault!" The nervous system doesn't care, it's just a worker bee, and it does what it's told to do. If you tell the worker bee the Old Story, it will begin to work on keeping you there; if you tell it the New Story, it will move toward that.

While it's clear optimistic thinking is basic to a strong mental state, it is not as easy as popular media might lead us to believe. Of course, we'd all like to think optimistically and many of the coaching sessions in this book can help including Mental Training 101, Spinning the Story, Changing Your Ringtone, and Asking the Can shift positive perception to optimistic. But while the power of this simple idea is still one of the foundations to moving forward, what's tricky about just thinking optimistically is that the pessimist inside us all does not just lie down and disappear, it's pushed further into the brain/body manifesting as pimples, muscle pulls, anger, and outbursts.

We need an adaptation. The very simple trick is to understand that pessimistic thoughts are powerful because they render us powerless. In order to let them go, we need to gain that power back. The way to do this is to remember that thinking like a pessimist is actually a choice we make. There's a guy at one of the firms I work with who is particularly adept at being a pessimist. At one point this year he was up $500,000. When he started to lose money, he dropped down to $300,000, which actually isn't that much to lose in the game these guys are playing. I pointed out that if he was head of the firm, he'd be down $1.2 million right now. Rather than choosing to take the view of the optimist, he said, "Yeah but he can afford to have down days. If only I had that kind of money, I'd be fine." Because the pessimist had come out to play, he's onto the, "It's easy for the other guy" syndrome. If he can create enough space to realize how counterproductive the inner pessimist is, he just might find an optimistic story with which to replace it. But right now he's choosing the negative, which is increasing his powerlessness.

Negative thoughts are iterative. They spiral into "catastrophe" thinking that is often completely outside of the present moment. Without space from his negative thoughts, this guy at the fund will probably picture himself losing money until he gets fired, and winds up panhandling on 14th Street.

A while ago Greg, a fellow tennis player, called to say he was worried because he had to have hip surgery. He wanted to know how close to 100 percent I was after my hip replacement and how long it took to recover because he would "go crazy" if he wasn't playing tennis. Greg's negative thoughts were tripping into a pretty horrible future. Negative thoughts are catching, and he'd picked up some others along the way. He said someone had told him that the docs need to dislocate your hip during surgery. When he heard this, he remembered a movie he'd seen of a dead guy whose limbs were all dislocated and he couldn't shake the image.

"Good," I told him. "The best thing you could be doing is calling me up on the phone and telling me this. Now that you've said them aloud, you can get some space from them. Find a New Story about your hip, your health, and your surgery, and only choose thoughts that will support that New Story and make the surgery a better experience. Look at people who had easy recoveries and whose surgeries were a success. Don't watch videos of the surgery and let go of the image from the movie—that's a dead guy, it isn't you."

Letting go of a thought that doesn't help is not that tough. It is so simple that people can't believe it can work. Closers— baseball pitchers whose job it is to close the game are trained in letting go of pessimistic thoughts. They learn to bring to the game an imaginary garbage pail that has written on the side, "useless thoughts for now." If they give up a hit and put the win at risk, the closer might think, "Oh, no, I am letting down the team. They are going to pull me from the game." But they have been taught to talk to that thought, "Hey, not now. I am putting you in the garbage pail and will pick you up on the way out of the park." Hard to believe it works. Give it a try. You will be amazed.

You want to catch pessimism before it drowns you. And getting a little space to notice negative thoughts will help. You can write them down, and find the Old Story contained there, tell them to a friend or simply sit in silence and ask yourself what thoughts are pulling you down. For instance, just realizing you forgot the milk on your way home and telling yourself, "I'm so forgetful" is the pessimist coming out to play. We tend to default to a negative way of thinking. Instead of obsessing about forgetting, notice it as a story. As it dissipates plug in "Oh I'm so glad I remembered the bread." Essentially to become a master of optimism, we need to have the intention to be free of the inner pessimist. It's not that pessimistic thoughts don't arise, it's that we don't engage with them. We need to practice. And we need to practice a lot. If you tend to be a pessimist, there are many opportunities throughout the day to remind yourself of the choice to be an optimist. Your New Story is one of optimism. You signed a contract that said you can be what you want to be for this moment, you can. You can choose to think like an optimist.

Remember that negative thoughts can pose as positive: *"Keeping my kid from failing"* or *"Keeping my family out of the poorhouse"* or *"Trying not to get fired."* When Ghandi was pursuing an independent state for India, he didn't say, "Down with British Rule," he said, "Freedom for India." In the movie *The Pursuit of Happyness*, Chris Gardner, a single dad who had lived through an abusive, violent childhood was so poor he and his son had to spend the night in church shelters, did not state his New Story as "getting out of poverty;" he said it was "financial independence."

Out of all the thoughts that come our way, why choose the Old Story? Once we know the thought was a choice, we can let it go and allow it to dissipate, and then send New Story thoughts into the void that's left. This is why we write our Old Story before we write the new one. When you write out the Old Story—those negative thoughts that feel so true— you are able to get some distance from that story and that space allows you to put positive thoughts in their place. Don't be afraid to think optimistically about your New Story. Sure, you may be disappointed sometimes when you find yourself not living it to its fullest, but disappointment is not that lasting. And there's very minimal short-term risk in an optimistic view. You gain the upside and minimize the downside. Look at that thought you are focusing on. Is that the thought you want to choose when there are so many thoughts to notice? Strange and simple as that sounds, by creating that space between you and your thought, it tends to dissipate, making room for a positive replacement.

SESSION TIP

The Big But: But when I am being optimistic, I feel like I'm in denial. I am telling myself a lie.

Try This On For Size: Always agree with your mind when it starts saying everything is bunch of bull; the agreeing often stops the mind in its track. Yes, everything is made up, but there are some positive slivers of sunshine amongst the debris. Make it a game to find the happy tracks through the minefield.

CHAPTER 15

Shoshin

In the beginner's mind there are many
possibilities, in the expert's mind there
are few.

—SHUNRYU SUZUKI

L ast week I saw rock legend Leon Russell perform. He's been playing the blues for more than 50 years, and when I watched him, it kind of felt like he was just going through the motions. He had done these songs so often that he was doing them from a distance. Even the between song raps seemed like they were words from the past. And then this week I went and saw Taj Mahal, who has been playing and singing the blues for 50 plus years. But what a different experience. Every note he played had a sense of electricity, what the Chinese call wu wei, a state in which our actions are effortlessly in alignment and totally natural. It was a wow. We were swept up. He was textbook *shoshin,* doing songs he had done hundreds of times as if it was the very first time.

The term *shoshin*, meaning "beginner's mind" was made popular by Shunryu Suzuki, a Japanese monk who wrote *Zen Mind, Beginner's Mind,* one of the best-loved Zen classics. When Shunryu first came to the United States, he used to say that Americans were wonderful to teach because they had beginner's mind. Shunryu died in 1971, and I wonder if he would think the same now, when we are constantly on our phones, taking pictures of sights instead of actually enjoying them. He believed in doing one thing at a time, as a way to cultivate this childlike state of the beginner's mind. If you've ever seen a puppy or a child playing, you are witnessing beginner's mind, as every ant hill and piece of scotch tape is brand new. When we are in beginner's mind, even mundane tasks are filled with wonder.

Today everyone is touting expertise as the holy grail, but does expertise feel alive? Is it exciting? Do you get to feel that brand new, falling in love for the first time feeling when you consider yourself an expert? The moments in our lives that are the most special are so because we are experiencing them as if for the very first time. Our first kiss. Falling in love. Writing our first word. The day our first child goes to school. Graduations. Catching your first wave as a surfer. Lying on the hood of the car on a summer night, looking out to the universe and feeling the vastness of it all. Simply feeling the warmth of the sun on our face. Little things we rarely notice are available to us all day, every day.

Gerry Marzorati was one of my more fascinating clients, a *NY Times Magazine* editor who, at 57, realized he had stopped improving. He was already good and skilled at what he did and he was just going through the motions. In his younger days he'd improved as a writer, an editor, a piano player. He grew as a son and as a spouse. But as he got older he leveled out. He wanted to rediscover growing at something to find that newness of life. He had always played tennis at his club and felt that he was pretty fit and played decently. But he wanted to be better, to play senior tournaments.

We played together at a club on Long Island, and he had good energy; he was eager and very interested, with good enthusiasm. He hit a good ball and was pretty consistent. We rallied and most of the rallies ended with him making an error by trying something that was on the edge of his ability. After each error, he berated himself, as many do, not yet realizing the consequences of negative self-talk.

After playing I asked him some probing questions. Why do you want to play tournaments? Why do you play tennis? What do you want to take away from a playing session? How do you think of competition? Do you love to play or do you just love winning? He hadn't thought much about this. He had invested more in lessons on strokes, techniques, and strategy. As he started to reveal himself, his Old Story took shape. *Competition makes me anxious. I am impatient and go for too much too soon. I don't like beating people because I'll be viewed as a bad guy. My focus is erratic especially when leading in a set or match. I lose faith in this game too quickly.*

We flipped his story and he got to work. He wrote each part in a better, more positive way so that he could move in that direction, and be a better player. He never lost enthusiasm. He totally bought in to the storytelling method. After he wrote the New Story, he used his writer's eye to pay attention to what was happening on the court when playing, he would spot the moments that his Old Story was operating as a default way and catch himself going along with it. He printed out his story and he read it. Every morning, every evening. Before he played. He began to notice the moments when his Old Story was operating as his default way, and he started to catch himself going along with it. And he would fight the Old Story with his New Story voice.

But as we continued to work, he lost the wow factor. The newness that created those high levels of excitement, awareness, and commitment began to wear off, and everything from his tennis game to his exciting New Story began to feel routine. So I told about *shoshin,* how to go back to beginner's mind. To make that his intention. To play and practice in *shoshin.* "Every time you go on the court, think about everything you don't know yet. What questions might you have? What are you curious about? When you hit the ball, hit it as if it's the first time you ever made contact with it. Keep your eye on it as if this was the very first time you were on the court."

We talked about practicing *shoshin* in small ways every day, like at dinner, take a bite of something as if it is the first time you ever ate that food. When at home, listen to your wife's voice as though it is the first time you have ever heard it. Get curious about how your feet feel when you are walking. See how far the elevator button really goes in. On the court, with your wife, at work, see things as for the first time.

Gerry went on to improve. He played and got crushed in some big tournaments but he kept moving forward toward his New Story. One step at a time. *Kaizen.* And it was joyful work for him. One day he called me to tell me that he had won a match in a tournament that he never would have won if not for his New Story.

Gerry's biggest strength and his largest liability was that he was an expert. He'd lost the ability to be a beginner, and that's probably why he intuitively wanted to play tennis again, but unfortunately simply starting something new isn't always enough. We need to learn to stay beginners, even when we get practiced at something, even when something is old hat.

When I was teaching tennis at the beginning, I used to teach this mantra from Timothy Gallwey's classic book, *The Inner Game of Tennis*. Bounce hit. Bounce hit. This became thematic for me. When I gave someone a lesson, same day, same time every week, I'd tell them we were going to work on bounce hit. "When the ball bounces, say bounce and when I make contact you say hit, and that will occupy your mind like listening to the music instead of trying to focus on the steps. The fourth lesson would come along, and they'd say, "Hey, aren't we going to do something else?" "No," I'd tell them "because you don't have this yet. Once you have this we can go to the next thing. You will have found beginner's mind and all else will come more easily."

Here's why I taught in that way: our minds start to take for granted the things with which we become most comfortable— when the key is actually to keep making the experience brand new over and over again. To pay attention. When you can feel like a beginner it helps you focus again.

As Emily Pereira, founder of the Be the Beginner brand says, "In this fast-paced world of experts and insane busyness, we've lost track of our most prized resource, the one thing that can turn it all around and hand you sparkling success on a silver platter—reawakening The Beginner inside. It's widely known that orchestra musicians who are instructed to make their performance new in subtle ways not only enjoy themselves more but audiences actually prefer those performances."

"When we're there at the moment, making it new, it leaves an imprint in the music we play, the things we write, the art we create, in everything we do," says Harvard professor and mindfulness expert Ellen Langer. "Once you recognize that you don't know the things you've always taken for granted, you set out of the house quite differently. It becomes an adventure in noticing—and the more you notice, the more you see."

As you read this book, you are experiencing *shoshin,* you are a child in the New Story world. You may notice, if you have worked with any of these coaching sessions before that you find yourself saying, oh! I know all about that. But each moment we are different from the one before, our perceptions change, our cells shift, so even something that feels familiar, when experienced as brand new, can create monumental shifts. You aren't supposed to have "gotten" it yet, the world is always yours to explore.

Why cultivate *shoshin*? When we cultivate the beginner's mind, everything we do comes alive. We experience freedom from judgment. Our critic dies. Our ego floats away. We return to our more natural states of connection and access the intelligence of the universe. Life becomes a wow in every way. Effort becomes effortless. Clarity arrives. We make better decisions as we move into our left brain of creativity, instinct, and non-analytic thinking. Our muse has room to climb inside us. The pieces begin to make sense even if things are in chaos. We become detached from righteous thinking.

What don't you know? Play like it is the first time you ever played and play like it is the last day of your life. Experts may have the best answers, but beginners have the best questions. What we don't know is exciting. We don't actually know how far the elevator button goes in. We don't know its feel on our fingertip, the sound of it rising, even our daughter's laugh.

Have you ever really listened to the quality of it?

SESSION TIP

The Big But: But I am a jaded adult, there's no way I can possibly get back to a child's mind; I am a failure at this.

Try This On For Size: What is it like to feel like a failure at getting into beginner's mind? Where do you feel it in your body? How does the world look when you feel you cannot see it from a child's point of view? Answering those questions is a way to experience Shoshin.

CHAPTER 16

Focus

Every time I feel I'm losing my own focus,
I ask myself one question: What am I
trying to accomplish?

—Steve DeMasco, Kung Fu Master

Be the ball.

—Bill Murray, in the film Meatballs

I began to live in focus. Fighting off
thoughts of the past and future.

—Mihaly Csikszentmihalyi,
speaking about how he survived
his prison time during World War II

Focus. Focus. Focus. Everybody wants it. Athletes. Business
people. Students. Parents want it, and they want their kids to
have it. Spouses want their partners to have *more* of it. Coaches
tout it as one of the most important tools for being at the top of
your game. Jack Canfield's *The Power of Focus: What the World's*

Greatest Achievers Know about the Secret to Financial Freedom & *Success* has sold millions of copies. The best moments of our life are those that happened when we were focused. Falling in love. The birth of our children. Graduation days. That perfect golf shot. The Grand Canyon or Yosemite. Focus is the ever elusive zone where every decision is right and every move is easy. A state of effortless effort. Focus is a fantastic tool to get to your New Story. But what is it, really?

In my early days of teaching tennis I worked hard to get my students focused. I named my business The Sports Focus Institute and was known as the "focus coach." For many hours a week I was trying to first understand what focus was and then trying to access the state. I had experiences when teaching, writing, or playing where I was focused, not through effort but through being fully engaged with what I was doing. But it felt tricky to get there. I kept using force, feeling that focus involved lots of mental effort.

And then, at a seminar I held for golfers, an attendee volunteered that Ben Hogan had said, "When standing over the ball, it is necessary to empty one's mind." I was skeptical, thinking, "That's a great idea but how in the world do you empty your mind?"

Some activities draw you to this state of no-thought because without it, you could die. My friend Bo Parfet, who has summited the seven highest mountains in the world told me, "You have to focus or you fall, there is no middle ground. If you have a very sick child, focus floods in, there is no choice. Driving in a fierce snowstorm. This is what happened to me when Carol got a second cancer, when she said "I won't survive this." Drawn to a state of instant focus . . . or fall.

But when the situation is not life threatening, how do we

become free of thoughts? Hogan's words kept popping up for me. And somewhere I knew he was right; when Stephen Curry makes a behind-the-back pass, he's not consciously thinking "How can I pass the ball?" If he did, he would interrupt his flow-like state and probably throw the ball into the stands. He was in what Hogan calls "a mind that was free of thoughts." But how did it come about?

The lesson came to me when I finally understood that focus wasn't something we do, it's how we do something, it's a state of being. And while there were seemingly random moments of focus, in order to make focus a state of being, we have to learn how to approach life.

Ali knocked to the mat by Frazier, head spinning but getting up to fight back. That's focus.

Climbing Everest but not reaching the summit because the weather turned against you and yet still planning your next ascent, that's focus.

Focus is Djokovic in the US Open Finals, one point away from losing the game at break point. He only had twenty seconds to refocus. Twenty seconds to enter into an incredible emotional environment of quiet and go back to the next point. That's focus.

One of the pioneers of the scientific study of happiness, Mihaly Csikszentmihalyi, mentions focus when he tells the story of being put in an Italian prison during World War II. During that time, when his relatives and friends had been killed in Budapest, his brother had died in combat, and his mother had been forced into a labor camp in Siberia, he discovered the game of chess. For hours he would focus within a reality that had clear rules and goals. He went on to write books about the experience of what he called "flow." His book Flow: The Psychology of Optimal Experience influenced world leaders and coaches from former President Bill Clinton to British Prime Minister Tony Blair to Dallas Cowboys coach Jimmy Johnson, who used Flow in preparing for the 1993 Super Bowl.

Mihaly conducted an experiment known as The Beeper Study. A group of teenagers were given beepers that went off randomly during the day. They were asked to record their thoughts and feelings at the time of the beeps. Most of the entries indicated that the teens were unhappy, but Csikszentmihalyi found that when their energies were focused on a challenging task, they tended to be more upbeat. It's true. Focus on something, and you create happiness. Focus on your New Story, by reading it day after day, and practicing the tools, and you will find, as many before you have, that you feel more productive, blissed out, relaxed, and excited about life.

Focus is playing your best. It is following through on a plan or working toward achieving a goal. Focus is staying committed to the bigger picture. Focus is staying on track. While focus sometimes arises at random moments, sustained focus arises when you become so fully engaged with and committed to an activity, you are no longer thinking. When we focus like this, our basal ganglia, that super computer at the top of the spine, takes over. This super computer is responsible for breathing, pumping blood, digestion, and a host of other actions that keep our bodies running. It is also responsible for mastery and flow. When you are no longer learning something, when you have done it again and again, the basal ganglia takes over, and when that happens, the parts of the brain responsible for worrying, future tripping, and figuring calm down and go to sleep. You are just in your mastery. No effort. No trying. No thought. Just being. That's why it's so fascinating to watch people who have been at their passion forever get out there and practice it: dancers, musicians, athletes. They kept at it for years, and now they are in a complete state of focus. That's what focus is: there's no separation between who you are and what you are doing. You are one with it.

But if we fall out of focus, what do we do? The truth is, it's easy to fall out of focus. Distraction is like a drug, an addiction. David Rock, co-founder of the NeuroLeadership Institute and author of *Your Brain at Work* says our brain's reward circuit lights up when we multitask. We get an emotional high from it. Of course it also drops our IQ, we make more mistakes, become less detail-oriented, and have a shorter fuse. In short, not having focus can lead you right back into an Old Story.

So how do you reboot your focus? While whole books have been written on focus, I find one thing to be exceedingly effective, and it's so incredibly simple, you may risk dismissing it. Don't. At any time of day, ask yourself this very potent question, "Am I focused?"

This question creates space. Quiet space where you can check out where your mind is. As soon as you ask it, you find yourself moving back on the path. The beauty of the reboot is that it is instantaneous. I used to think focus was a huge amount of effort, work. But it just takes that one, quick question. Even though it might only work for a moment, we have the choice of another moment and another and eventually the moments flow together and become a state of being. Until we drop out again. And then, we ask the question again, and another moment awaits; and focus, that beautiful wild wonderful feeling of being truly committed, comes into view.

SESSION TIP

The Big But: I've never been good at focusing. I have ADD; my mind tends to go a million directions in a moment.

Try This On For Size: Make a list of three times when you've been superbly focused. This could be when you were studying for a test at college, giving birth, or learning to drive. Now take the next step. If you focused once, you can focus again; this will give you fodder for the part of the brain that believes in the can't.

When in real doubt, see Chapter 19 on Asking the Can.

CHAPTER 17

Redefine Winning

I've missed more than 9,000 shots in
my career. I've lost almost 300 games.
Twenty-six times I've been trusted to take
the game winning shot and missed. I've
failed over and over and over again in my
life. And that is why I succeed.

—MICHAEL JORDAN

How big is our definition of winning? If our idea of winning only includes winning the match, getting that plum job, having your child get into the best college, scoring a date with that special someone, or making partner at that firm, you might be at risk of feeling like the biggest loser.

We want the obvious, more visible win because it's easier to focus on the external: the better job, losing weight, making more money. When I first started playing tennis, I didn't know yet about the power of New Stories and it was all about winning and losing for me. Who I was, if I was a success or failure, had to do only with results. But those results weren't really filling my bucket. So I started to make up some other ways in which I could win. I started to search for what I could pull out of the experience that felt like a win. I would share them with my students. I am not even sure that, at the beginning, I believed that these new wins would fill that bucket but I persisted. I began to have an awareness that each match had something in it that was positive and was moving me toward a New Story in tennis. Playing fair, keeping calm, pushing through resistance—these were all big wins too.

Finding the win often means looking at some pieces of your New Story. If a trader's New Story is *being accepting and adaptable,* then his win on a given day might be that he was able to accept the market volatility or to adapt to the changing market moves. Seeing the win might lead him to trade better and watch his PNL improve. Your New Story is a broader win. Even if you have a bad day, your salary doesn't go up, you don't win the award or get the contract, if you lived any part of your New Story, you can consider that a win. So, if John McEnroe, who was a notorious hot head on the court, decided to redefine winning as being those times when he exercised patience and good sportsmanship, he may have felt like a winner even more of the time. And feeling like a winner is really helpful when you are working on your performance in anything you do. Winning feelings promote solution-based thinking and optimism as well as just feeling good.

Our definition of win needs to be bigger. Billie Jean King was obviously a great tennis player who won many many championships, but she is not known for these championships. She is known for changing women's place in sports. She is known for standing up and saying women wouldn't play anymore unless they made the same amount of money as men. She was one of the strongest manifestations of the women's lib movement. When Bobby Riggs chauvinistically said that the women's game was inferior, and he could easily beat the best woman player in the world and claimed, "It's not even a match." She carried the banner for all women and in the most watched event in sport's history at the time, she beat him. She changed how the world viewed women's sports and women's empowerment. That was her win. A far greater win than any number of trophies. If you said to her right now, looking back on your life, what was your greatest accomplishment, it probably wouldn't be her twenty Wimbledon titles. She would likely say that she created influence in the world. That she shifted the world.

When Billie Jean told me to make sure my students knew that it was not about the trophies, I smugly said, "that's easy for you to say, you've won 39 grand slams." Her answer was quick: "That's why you should believe me. I have seen the view from the top of the mountain." When I wound up winning the world championship, I understood what she meant. While that win was big, the biggest wins were the broader ones: practicing relaxation in the midst of a perceived stressful situation was a win, finding new ways to hit the ball or new places on the court, developing a sense of purpose for each shot; the engagement itself was a win, being faced with failure and giving full effort at pushing it away was a win, pushing my limits, squeezing out on more drop of focus, effort, or energy. Being a good loser and winner is winning big. Anytime I made my time on the court meaningful and special, I felt that I'd won.

I still fail at things on some days, and I win on other days. But the joy of working on the details and "winning" in some way every day has kept me engaged, focused, interested, happy. I feel I am a better player today than 10 and even 20 years ago, and that's a huge payoff.

The thing about external winning is that on any given day, you can do all the parts right and still not get the win. In some activities if one person wins, then someone loses. Waiting for only good results to get yourself to feel good can be a certain way to be unhappy much of the time. If your win is personal, you have an array of wins at your fingertips. What does winning mean to you, in this moment? In this day? In your career? In your marriage? With your kids? This often boils down not to what you want to get, but who you want to *be*. Your New Story. When we redefine the win as elements of the New Story: patience, acceptance, focusing on the game rather than results, being a role model, then you notice that you do "win" more at work, on the court, and in your relationships.

SESSION TIP

The Big But: Maybe there are invisible wins, but I get paid for good results, not making a good effort or behaving well.

Try This On For Size: The fantastic thing about redefining the win is that when you see the small wins, even among what we call the "losses," we tend to begin to win more. Why? It's the reticular activating system in the brain. What we pay attention to grows. When we begin to see wins everywhere, we begin to win more and more, on a larger and larger scale.

CHAPTER 18

Mission/Driver/ Your Big Why

When you are inspired by some great
purpose, some extraordinary project,
all your thoughts break their bonds:
Your mind transcends limitations, your
consciousness expands in every direction,
and you find yourself in a new, great,
and wonderful world. Dormant forces,
faculties and talents, become alive, and
you discover yourself to be a greater
person by far than you ever dreamed
yourself to be.

—PATANJALI

What are we working so hard for? Why does it really matter? For years companies have been developing mission statements to answer those questions. Google wants to "organize the world's information and make it universally accessible and useful." Life is Good exists to "Spread the power of optimism." IKEA wants to make "everyday life better for their customers."

When Stephen R. Covey wrote *The 7 Habits of Highly Effective People,* he advised his readers to create their own mission statements. And that concept took off. You can find the personal mission statements of Oprah, Richard Branson, and Amanda Steinberg, among many others online. Jim Loehr says missions are the roots, of our actions. He often tells a story about a city in Florida where they planted a bunch of palm trees; there was a storm right after the planting and the roots weren't deep enough yet to fight off the challenge, so the trees fell. The mission is the roots, what is growing underneath the branches and leaves of one's life. When we have a strong mission, we won't fall. The mission is the heart of your New Story, it's the engine, driving your actions with the same relentless, day-after-day, commitment to keep going through good and bad, success and failure.

When Victor Frankl was in the concentration camps during World War II, his mission was to survive in order to tell the story so that it might never happen again. He worked for jailers and picked people to go to the ovens, he went without food and clothing in the freezing cold, he survived because he had a mission: to tell his story. Missions are the ultimate motivators.

People often ask how to find the mission. If you don't have a mission, don't give it too much thought, your New Story will be enough. Your New Story might be, "I have deep and clear purpose in my life." That, in and of itself, can have you growing deeper roots. "My stories show me the path to my mission." Remember, it is your life and you get to make up the rules. In essence, what is driving you? For my client who had night eating as part of her Old Story, we had to ask this question: *What was she trying to give herself when she ate at night? What was the mission she was tiring to accomplish?* The answer? To nurture herself. Because nurturing herself might have been to eat three donuts before going to sleep, the next question was: *How can I nurture myself even better than I am now?* She can take a warm bath instead of eating. She can call a friend. She can make a cup of tea and write her gratitudes for the day.

In my own case, I was driven to win because it felt good. Why did it feel good? Because I had low self-esteem, and I wanted to be seen. Why did I want to feel seen? *I want to feel powerful. I want to be well liked. I want to escape loneliness.* Now you are onto the real juice. *And you can ask yourself, what else besides the win can make me feel powerful?* Now you have a mission-driven life.

Once I understood my mission was to be seen, and how motivating that was, I asked myself *how* I wanted to be seen. I wanted the best version of myself to be seen. The win was a *what,* the best version of myself was a *who.* The *who* you want to be is always going to be more powerful than the *what* you want. What you want is going to change. My mission morphed into wanting to show up as the best version of myself. Every action and decision I made was based on that. Once you know your purpose, it tends to change your behavior. If a kid isn't acting politely on the playing field, you may not be able to change his behavior by telling him to be polite, but if you ask him, "What do you want people to say about you off the field?" This may begin to change him. Asking this question—*How do you want people to talk about you?*—is a great way to find the mission. A new friend who has Parkinson's disease just shared with me that when he is feeling defeated he thinks about what he would say if he did a Ted Talk called, "I love my Parkinson's." That is how he finds his mission.

What makes you feel good? Look at things that you have already accomplished, what was leading you to accomplish this? When you are working with your true mission, there's an energetic feeling of effortlessness. The mission draws us, it doesn't push us. It never has to do with another person's idea of what we should do. Don't ask "am I being what others think I should be or am I being what I should be?" No should's at all. The better question is "who do I want to be?" It needs to make *you* feel good, that's the motivator, a contentedness at the end of the day. If it's not your true mission, it feels like work. When you truly find your mission, the things that are necessary to complete the mission come easily to you. The mission becomes the coach, taking you where you want to go.

In 2004 I had a chance to test this mission. I was on an amazing streak of tennis. I was 56 years old and had won the National Grass 55 and Over Championships, both the singles and doubles, for two consecutive years. The day after the tournament ended, my teammates and I headed to Philadelphia to play in the Senior Davis Cup, and then we were on to the ITF World Championships. I was seeded #1, the favorite. I was excited that the World Championships were being played in the United States on the grass, my favorite playing surface.

But six months earlier, as I was filling out my entry for the Worlds, the September date made me take a second look. The Jewish holidays, Rosh Hashanah and Yom Kippur, occur each year on a different date, and always take place in September or October. Sure enough, when I looked at my calendar, my inkling was confirmed, the finals of the World Championships were scheduled to be played on Yom Kippur.

I am proud of being Jewish and especially proud of being a Jewish tennis player. One tradition that my family brought me up with was that we never did anything on Yom Kippur. It is the holiest day and even someone not very religious wouldn't go to work and would fast. That is the bare minimum.

So I wrote the ITF, the international governing body of tennis and asked them if they realized the tournament finals were scheduled on the holiest Jewish holiday? This was a day that many of my faith do not engage in regular daily activities, like playing tennis. I didn't suggest I would be in the finals, as many things need to go really well for that to happen. It's a very hard thing to do. But since the event was in Philadelphia, there were many age groups playing and there was a sizable Jewish population there, there was a pretty good chance one of the finalists might be faced with the problem. They countered by saying they couldn't avoid all holidays. If it was a problem for me, I shouldn't play.

Well, I wanted to play, and I didn't really think it was going to be a problem. I had been a finalist in the World Championship several years earlier but didn't really think I'd be one again. Still, when I let myself daydream, I had to ask myself whether I would play on Yom Kippur or not. Complicating the decision was the possibility that I could achieve the World #1 ranking if I won the title. This ranking was a dream of mine, and it had actually felt within reach over the last couple of years. But it wasn't my mission. My mission had gone way beyond "being seen" and external goals. It had gone way beyond winning. Now my mission was about integrity and courage and being willing to sacrifice the external win for internal growth. My mission was about to be tested.

When I got to the tournament, I started winning. I won all

the way up to the semi-finals. If I won one more match, I'd have a chance to be the top-ranked player in the world. I had been telling myself the story about my mission for months. And now I was in the position to follow through. That afternoon, I went into the ITF office and said to the officials, "Hey guys, remember that letter I sent you six months ago? About the Jewish holiday that is coming up?" They were surprised, they hadn't realized that their #1 seed was the one who had sent it.

I told them if I won the next day, I wouldn't play on the day scheduled and asked if there was anything they could do to move the finals up.

No. If I didn't want to play, I shouldn't play.

Although I very much wanted to win my match to get to the finals, knowing that I was playing for my mission rather than for a win had a huge calming effect on what happened when I got on the court the next day. I was playing to win to maintain my personal integrity. To take a stand. To honor the memory of my parents and to be a role model for my daughters. I played free. My mission carried me. I felt my parents there with me. Supporting me. Cheering for me quietly. Not for the tennis victory but for the personal victory.

I won the match. After I defaulted, the ITF officials informed me that there was a rule that "any player that does not play a scheduled match without a written medical excuse would be penalized the prize money, the medal, and the ranking points." I gave away the World #1 ranking to support my mission. My biggest win in tennis was in a match that I never even played.

There's a reason the mission is called the North Star. The mission becomes one of the best decision making aids you have, it's a compass that helps lead you out of rough patches, helps you decide how to be in the world and what choices are right for you.

There's no doubt that having a big mission can provide motivation to do whatever it takes, and in some ways your New Story is your mission. Or your mission is contained in your New Story. But just like it's good to have mini-stories, it is also good to have bite-sized missions. You've heard it before, it's undeniably true: life is a series of moments. We can infuse each moment with mission. Our missions into incremental small steps. The mission might simply be, *Today I will be patient.* You may approach a conversation with a client, a co-worker, a spouse, your daughter, and ask yourself what your mission is, *To be a better listener.* While you are drinking your coffee or brushing your teeth you might ask yourself, *What's my mission today?* You may have a different mission for your marriage than for your business. Your mission can be simple: The Dalai Lama said: *Ask yourself what you can do to make a difference in one person's life today.*

The mission tells you what strategy to use. If your greater north star is integrity, then when the cashier at the market gives you change from a twenty when you only gave them a ten, you let them know and return it.

Your mission may be freedom rather than money, in which case you may not want to pick up more clients even though more clients means more money. If your core mission is freedom, you can begin to throw kindling on it. What does it mean to have freedom in your relationships? Your health? Your finances? Your career? A mission helps you stay motivated and creates a solid foundation that will drive your life. Without a mission, it can be difficult to make these huge decisions in life, difficult to decide on a personal brand, difficult to solve moral dilemmas, difficult to follow through on your New Story without the sense of a larger, greater force at work. You'll know it when you find it.

It's the one that makes you feel like you are flying.

SESSION TIP

The Big But: But the whole idea of a mission seems too big to me. I struggle to understand how to even create one.

Try This On For Size: You can actually have a mission in any part of your life. Starting small (Kaizen, Chapter 13) can help tremendously. Try writing a small mission first in preparation for the bigger one.

My mission today is to be curious by asking at least one question of someone at work. My mission for doing the dishes is to only think about the present. My mission for putting my child to bed is to only focus on him, not to hurry him and to have patience. Once you've succeeded in these immediate missions, then you can move on to bigger missions—like being a true friend or being an extraordinary parent.

CHAPTER 19

Asking the Can

You are braver than you believe,
stronger than you seem and smarter than
you think.

—Winnie-the-Pooh

Nothing is impossible, the word itself says
'I'm possible'!

—Audrey Hepburn

M y Dad was someone who went against the norm. He loved
to prove that he could do whatever he wanted. He was
always "asking the can" putting full effort into answering the
question "why can I do this?" After enlisting in the Navy at the
beginning of WWII, he saw that the Marines were "the real men
fighting the war" and switched over. At the time, there were very
few Jewish Marines, but he had a quiet confidence that made
him a leader, and he worked his way up the ranks to captain.

After the war he worked in a department store, managing sales people. Knowing he could do much more, he took a big risk and used his and my mom's savings to buy a lumberyard. He followed his vision and turned it into one of the two largest concrete companies on Long Island. In those days the concrete business was mostly run by Italians, mobsters, and teamsters. When the teamsters went on a wildcat walkout strike and there were no drivers for the trucks, my dad worked to bust the union by hiring scabs—non-union drivers—and leading them across the picket line. At dinner one night he told my sister and me that we were going to be getting rides to school rather than taking the bus. At the time he didn't tell us that the drivers were bodyguards.

He'd played baseball and basketball for Brooklyn College. Once we moved to Long Island, he found tennis as a way to stay in a competitive game. He introduced me to the game when I was 12. During his final days, he would watch me play as I was just beginning to compete, and he was always positive and proud. He asked the *can,* and he expected me to ask it, too. How *can* I be good at this? He never spoke of why he couldn't. He's the one who gave me the can. I learned how to use this valuable question, and it has led me to create big stories. My tennis, my career, finding new love, and this book.

Henry Ford failed and went broke five times before he succeeded. Twenty-seven publishers rejected Dr. Seuss. Jack London received 600 rejection slips. R. H. Macy failed seven times before his store in New York City caught on. Stan Smith was told he was too awkward and clumsy to be a ball boy, although he went on to win Wimbledon, the U. S. Open, and eight Davis Cups. Olaudah Equiano went from slavery to becoming a celebrated author who changed the way the British thought about emancipation. All of them asked the can. Michelangelo wrote,

"The greater the danger for most of us is not that our aim is too high, and we miss it, but that it is too low and we reach it." He asked the can, and is considered one of the greatest and most prolific artist of all times.

When I first wanted to move from sports mental coaching to business coaching, I asked people on Wall Street how I might do it. Typically they would tell me why I couldn't. *You don't know this business, people will see you as a sports coach, you don't have the degree you need.* The problem was, I knew all that. It is easy to know why you *can't*. I wanted to know the *can*.

The worst can'ts are not from external sources. They come from within you. And while the external can'ts might hit you hard, it's the internal judges, whispering in your ear, that can provide the knockout punch to your dreams.

But even if you have failed again and again and again, if you ask the can, you may wind up shifting history, or at least living a completely New Story. Winston Churchill repeated a grade during elementary school and, later was placed in the lowest division of the lowest class. He failed the entrance exam to the Royal Military College twice and was defeated the first time he tried to serve in Parliament. When he became Prime Minister in his 60s he wrote, "Never give in, never give in, never, never, never, never—in nothing, great or small, large or petty—never give in except to convictions of honor and good sense. Never, Never, Never, Never give up."

Once we think we can't live our New Story, because of an injury, our genetic disposition, our age, the amount of money we have, and so on . . . we tend to lose energy, to back away from the dream of the New Story. Making a list of the cans, if only in your mind, can go a long way. Your history is a huge help here.

If you've finished a marathon, you can probably finish writing a book; if you've raised kids, chances are you can grow a pretty beautiful garden; if you built a successful financial foundation once, chances are you can build one up again; if you had one idea that turned profitable, chances are you'll have another.

Role models who have gone against all odds (some are listed above), are excellent resources for the can. But be ready, that can't voice tends to be pretty loud. That's the voice of the Old Story. Your mind's first default response may be to list the can'ts of the New Story. That's a survival instinct. If you are thinking an "I can't thought," asking the can is going to bring you a long way toward your New Story. Rather than, what can't I do, what can I do? This is often a very subtle shift, but it can change your whole life. As Nelson Mandela once said, "There is no passion to be found in playing small—in settling for a life less than what you are capable of living." This from a man who asked the can after 25 years in jail and became the first black president of a country once ruled by apartheid. You can.

SESSION TIP

The Big But: But I'm just being realistic when I think of the can'ts. I don't want to delude myself and find out that the can'ts are the real story.

Try This On For Size: Just about everything that you can do now, you couldn't do at one time. You might have been too young, too small, too afraid, or too unskilled. What if, when you were a child, you were stopped by this thought: I can't walk.

Luckily, you didn't have any negative thought systems in place yet, so you tried again and again until today you are up and walking around. Here you are now faced with something that feels like a can't, but just like walking, riding a bike, learning a foreign language, or driving a car, the can't of today turns into the can of tomorrow. Find your can.

CHAPTER 20

Mentors and Anti-Mentors

I'm Mr. Bad Example, intruder in the dirt
I like to have a good time, and I don't care
  who gets hurt
I'm Mr. Bad Example, take a look at me
I'll live to be a hundred, and go down in
  infamy!

—WARREN ZEVON

W e all have mentors—people who inspire us. They seem to exist to show us the blueprint of who we could be if we were living our best stories. Growing up, I was a skinny kid with a lot of fears, I wanted to be courageous and strong, and my models became characters from books and TV shows like Huck Finn, Robin Hood, King Arthur, the Hardy Boys, Spin and Marty, Superman, and The Lone Ranger. This may seem silly now, but authors of kids' books and creators of TV shows often build up a fictional character's great qualities, so what better place to find mentors who are living your New Story, or parts of that story? Even today I aspire to be like some of my favorite protagonists, each of whom have qualities to which I aspire: Dirk Pitt, Reacher, Bob "the nail" Swagger. They are my mentors, and I role-play them. These days many of my mentors are athletes: Federer, Nadal, Djokovic, Manning, Gretzky, Derek Jeter, Magic and Larry Bird.

Just knowing you admire someone isn't enough, it's about really picking apart what characteristics, specifically, you want to emulate (he's patient, he doesn't get flustered easily, he makes goals and keeps them, he's always learning something new), studying their outlooks, reactions, and responses create a road-map toward the New Story. Qualities that I aspire to bring into my life.

Looking at iconic, larger-than-life figures you often find a mentor was at the foundation of their success stories. Thanks to a rough-handed medical intern, a pair of forceps dragged Sly Stallone by his face into the world on July 6, 1946, severing the facial nerves in his eyelid and lips. Bullied at school he used muscular stars like Steve Reeves as role models and got into body-building. Weights cost more money than he had, so he pilfered heavy automobile parts out of the local junkyard and worked out with cinderblocks attached to a pole. Later, when he went out for film roles, he used that forceps incident to his advantage (see Chapter 11: Dancing with the Beast) and that soon-to-be-famous sneer help to type cast him as a tough guy. Stallone's used a ton of New Story tools to create a recipe of success including *finding the can* and *spinning the story*, but it all started with his use of role models to become stronger. Sully Sullenberger, who landed the US Airways flight in the Hudson River became a role model. The New York firemen and EMTs became heroic models in the face of 9/11.

As important as mentors are, the anti-mentor can be even more powerful. A few months ago a headline caught my eye: "Trainwreck Starlets Are the Anti-Role Models We Need, and Here's Why." The Cosmo.com article went on to say that role models are good for helping us to reach our goals, and anti-role models can "keep us from falling on our face." They mentioned Lindsay Lohan as a good example. When Bill Clinton made a poor choice with Monica Lewinsky in the Oval Office and lied about it, he became an anti-model. Tiger Woods became one of the most notorious anti-models when his personal life began to encroach on his incredible career as a golf player. Lance Armstrong leveraged his cancer battle to be seen as a model of positivity only to become an anti-model of the nth degree who will always be known as a cheater and liar. Bernie Madoff, so highly respected on Wall Street for so long, became the face of extraordinary deceit, stealing millions of dollars from trusting investors. Their mistakes and choices remind us to stay on the paths to our best stories.

I have a friend whose father was born with a silver spoon in his mouth and lost it all to a prescription drug habit and a propensity for self-indulgence. My friend used her father as an anti-model. "Whatever my father did, from never working hard, giving up on projects in the middle, zoning out on bad food and television, and using excuses, I would do the opposite." Today she's a successful business woman with a happy marriage and no bad habits.

Sometimes, though, the best anti-mentor is ourselves. In 1982, I was teaching high school history, had been married to my high school girlfriend for almost 15 years, was the father of two young daughters, and kept wondering about a different and better life for myself. And then one morning, I was on the Ed Koch Bridge, crossing the East River into New York City when I saw a billboard for a feature film. Kevin Kline, William Hurt, Tom Berenger, Glenn Close and Jeff Goldblum were starring in a film called *The Big Chill,* which would become one of our biggest baby boomer cult classics. It wasn't until I got closer that my world was exploded. The screenplay was by Larry Kasdan and Barbara Benedek. I'd distantly known Kasdan when I was at the University of Michigan, and Barbara was married to my college roommate, the founder of a successful Hollywood talent agency. This was the movie they'd told me about when I last saw them, based on my friends and me, Michigan students, 15 years later.

As I drove into the city I thought about what happened to my friends from the University of Michigan who had lived through the 60s. We who had arrived from our safe communities, without worries and been dropped into a cauldron of consciousness-raising, drugs, free love, rock and roll, and the anti-war movement. We were the first hippies. Bell-bottoms, long hair, sandals, and VW buses.

Where were we now?

I knew where *I* was. I was in a world of emotional pain, low self-esteem, and directionless. Thirty-three years old and still a hippy. The movie showed how different each of our lives had become. And for me, it was a wakeup call. It was time for a New Story. One year later I took a new job in the tennis business and had taken steps toward reinventing my coaching model. I got divorced. I fell in love. I got remarried. I started to fly.

How can you use mentors and anti-mentors while you are moving toward your New Story? After listing the characteristics of the people you admire, stick them in your New Story. Borrow the good stuff: *great father, always goes the distance for friends, knows how to reinvent himself.* As you are faced with big and small decisions during the day, pretend that you *are* them. What would they do in that situation? Imitation is one of the greatest innovators of greatness.

SESSION TIP

The Big But: But this doesn't work for me because all of these mentors had opportunities that I never had. I just can't identity with them.

Try This On For Size: Chances are that you have strengths that your role models don't have. We all have muscles we don't even realize are there because we use them so much that they become second nature.

Imagine that you serve as a role model to someone. What if they were to tell you, "*You have opportunities I never had, so I'm not even going to try.*" What would you tell them? Whatever you'd tell them, try that on yourself.

CHAPTER 21

Data Shmata

When you have exhausted all possibilities,
remember this: you haven't.

—THOMAS EDISON

Never let the odds keep you from pursuing
what you know in your heart you were
meant to do.

—SATCHEL PAIGE

One morning I was in the bagel shop and I saw a newscaster on television talking about a new study that said most people don't smile until 11:17 in the morning. When we hear data, our minds categorize and make order out of who we are. Okay, I know who I am, I am in the smaller group who smiles before 11:17 AM, or I am an outlier because certain things have happened to me. This data is true, and you either fall into a category or you don't, but either way you are categorized. This tendency of going with the flock gets in the way of our being genuine.

Data is static. If you hear that only 5 percent of women live with the kind of diagnosis you've been given, that category becomes a prison. It's extremely limiting and gets in the way of being able to change and morph into the New Story. In order to live our New Story, we have to believe that people, circumstances, diagnosis and situations shift.

Wired, MIT News, The New York Times, Harvard Business Review, and *INC* have all covered the immense problems data holds. *The New York Times* said it best when they wrote, "big data is prone to giving scientific-sounding solutions to hopelessly imprecise questions." In a 2014 *Harvard Business Review* article entitled "Eight (No, Nine!) Problems with Big Data," Thomas C. Redman, Ph.D., a data doctor, said knowledge workers spend 50 percent of their time correcting data mistakes. In short, data is not always accurate. Data is bent and spun and manipulated to evoke certain responses and reactions from consumers, clients, and patients.

When you are working on moving forward *never* let statistics convince you that they are *Truth.* There is always the power of one. That you can do what others have never done. Data guarantees nothing.

Years before I became a world champion in tennis, people said to me, *Hey, you didn't play tennis in college, and you didn't play on the tour, so you can't really ever be a high-ranking player.* My answer was always, "Why not?" Even if no one has ever done it before, I thought, I am going to be the one who does it. I believe in the power of *one.*

Of being the One.

Babe Ruth is famous for his record number of home runs, but for a long time, he also held the record for strikeouts, which outnumbered his home runs by over 600. Tom Landry, Chuck Noll, Bill Walsh, and Jimmy Johnson accounted for 11 of the 19 Super Bowl victories from 1974 through 1993. They also share the distinction of having the worst records of first-season head coaches in NFL history—they didn't win a *single* game.

Data might say a black man in 1930s' Berlin didn't stand a chance of success, but Jesse Owens won four Olympic gold medals in the 1936 Olympics and proved Hitler's pedagogy of Aryan superiority wrong. Data might have said that a deaf and blind girl in the late 19th century could never learn to read or write, but Helen Keller did both. Data might tell us that Pakistani women have no freedom and no opportunity but Malala Yousafzai, a Pakistani schoolgirl who survived being shot in the head, has become a global advocate for human rights, women's rights, and the right to education.

Sometimes we create data for ourselves, and we do not even realize we have done it, as illustrated by Tony Schwartz's book *What Really Matters*. Tony spent five years searching for guides on his road to wisdom. He studied meditation, biofeedback, peak performance training, right brain drawing, and more. On his search for the holy grail of self-improvement, what he found was that there were many ways, not just one, that could lead one on the path of self-discovery. There was no right way. Tony put a glitch in my own personal data by saying that there's only one way to get where you want to go. By no longer buying into the limitations of that personal data, I became free to explore unlimited ways to become a better coach, husband, father, friend, player, and human being in this world.

So, how do you combat the power of data? When you hear data that makes you feel hopeless or scared, you ask yourself:

"Is that really true?" "What is the source and is it pure?" "Am I believing it because I believe the person spouting it has more power, education, money, or experience than me?" "Could there be at least one person who defied this data?" "Could the next person be me?" What we forget is that there exists what I like to call the Data of One. Anyone can actually fall in anywhere. If it happened to one person, somewhere on the planet, it can happen to you. If one person survived your disease, you can survive it too. If one person descended Mt. Everest blind, you can too. If you think that you cannot live your New Story because it is too fantastic, too wonderful, why live like that? You are the data of one. The minute we have the ability to see beyond the terms data laid out for us, the moment you can find your way out of theory and into your own experience, that's when you begin to change rather than stay in stasis.

As Tony Schwartz says, "Let go of certainty. The opposite isn't uncertainty. It's openness, curiosity, a willingness to embrace paradox, rather than choose up sides." It's a commitment to reach outside of the confines that data traps us in and find our own power. Remember—you are unique, the data is not relevant.

You are the data of one.

SESSION TIP

The Big But: But without data, we wouldn't have a cure for polio or be able to put a man on the moon. I am someone who believes in using data to decide what to do. I like guarantees, and I believe in hard science.

Try This On For Size: Loving data is a good thing. Data is everywhere, it's extremely malleable and you can even make your own. If you are relying on data to tell you that you can or cannot do something, then you just need to make your own data. I am going to prove this can happen, by creating my own person data: I did this, so you can, too.

CHAPTER 22

The Watcher

Rather than being your thoughts and
emotions, be the awareness behind them.

—ECKHART TOLLE

We cannot undo the power of a
thought. We can, however, start thinking
about something else. We can become
aware in more and more moments of
where our minds are at and shift toward
thoughts that feel better than where we
currently stand.

—TIM KREMER

For a while I worked with a sweetheart hedge funder who was
having trouble moving toward his New Story. He had a pretty
gruff exterior, but underneath it all, he was fragile and, when I
met him, questioning the life he was living. He'd come from a
long line of depressives, and now that he was middle-aged, he

was going into what he called "the dark depression." He felt like there was no way to avoid it, he'd inherited the depression from his father, and even the best shrinks didn't know how to help him. Of course, this was an Old Story, a story that could be transformed and flipped, but he said his biggest problem after writing his New Story was trying to move toward it because his new voice was not as strong as his habitual old voice.

"That's understandable," I told him. "But did you know there's another part of you that's not the Old Story or the New Story? It's a part of you this is not story at all. That's the part that sees the depressed person you've been for so long and also sees the new light-hearted, optimistic person? This part of you is called The Watcher, and it's completely neutral. It doesn't care one way or another if you are following in your father's footsteps, as you put it, or in a state of optimism. The watcher is your home base, the part of you that's okay no matter what." The watcher just is.

It's difficult to switch from negative to positive in the snap of the fingers. When we get stuck in our Old Stories, it's important to be The Watcher, and from this neutral place, move again toward the qualities in the New Story. Some might call The Watcher "mindfulness," originally translated from the Buddhist Sanskrit term smrti, which means "to remember." What are we remembering? We are remembering that we are not the Old Story we are telling ourselves. We are remembering that there is a part of us that isn't shaming, telling stories, or creating drama.

Because bringing the word mindfulness to the table welcomes in a whole school of intense religious thought that has been talked about by Pali and Sanskrit scholars for centuries, I like to simplify it to The Watcher, less overwhelming, fewer strings attached that we can get tangled up in. You actually don't have to be really evolved to have a watcher inside you, even a really unconscious person has a watcher. When you recognize that there's a neutral watcher inside, you are taking a step toward your New Story. Your ability to enjoy your life and deal successfully with your problems increases. Being The Watcher can keep you balanced and set you free of triggers. The Watcher gives your body and your mind a rest.

It's not difficult to find your Watcher. If you close your eyes and sit for few minutes and watch your thoughts, you have become The Watcher. During those few minutes, notice other things, too: the sounds around you, the breath in and out, the places where your body seems tense, and then come back to the thoughts and notice the stories and drama around them, notice whether you are speaking positively to yourself or not. After those minutes, open your eyes and go back into your world.

When you are still in this way, the mind tends to blow all thoughts out. According to Case Western University psychology expert Richard Boyatzis, sitting in this way and being The Watcher can shift the parasympathetic nervous system, raise immune levels, slow the heart rate, alleviate stress, create renewed optimism, improve working relationships, and stoke compassion and creativity. It's like a miracle drug. Once I realized how mind-blowing this is, I went through the hedge fund like a bonfire to make sure every guy knew about it. Hedge funders who did this maintained better focus; were happy and more present at work and at home; played better golf, tennis, and squash; and made better decisions.

Why is this? Because unnoticed thoughts become our drivers. They become our negative missions, and we live to serve them. Just like when we write out our old stories, we see these counterproductive missions, when we become The Watcher, we see them in the moment. These counterproductive missions don't deserve psychology, they are just thoughts. Psychology is too big for them and feels too scary. They are just assumptions we've never really noticed. And The Watcher can de-escalate them. In order to engage with The Watcher, you can ask this simple question of the thoughts you see: Is that thought really true? Because the thought probably isn't true. It's just a thought, after all.

The watcher creates space between your reaction and your response. When you are struggling with something or someone, you can stop for a moment, and give your watcher a chance to notice the thoughts and beliefs around the situation. Your watcher is like another person who can give you some helpful insights.

If you are someone who labels yourself as type A, this act of non-doing, sitting in silence, seems complex. People ask, *Should I work on my posture? Should I observe my breath? Should I listen to music? What time of day?* I say, "Forget about all that. There are no rules to being The Watcher. Just make sure you are doing this every single day. It doesn't matter when. Wake up, check your emails, brush your teeth, and then for a few minutes sit, this is one place where there's non-doing. If you do it, a huge change will occur."

Of course, no one feels like they have spare minutes. They're always saying, *I don't have time during the day.* I say, "Do you have time to go to the bathroom?" And they say, *Well, yeah, but shouldn't I be doing it in a comfortable, quiet place?* And I tell them, "You *should* be closing your eyes for five minutes. Go ahead and do it in the bathroom, who knows what you are doing while you are sitting on the toilet?"

Know that there is a Watcher always there, helping you respond rather than react. Find the chill, the quiet in the storm, your Buddha within.

SESSION TIP

The Big But: But I have tried to meditate. It was terrible. I couldn't stop my thoughts for a moment. So how can I possibly be a Watcher? I won't be able to observe anything. **Try This On For Size:** If you've noticed that you can't stop your thoughts, you are already there. How did you know that? You watched; you observed that very thing. The more your watch, the more your thoughts will even out.

You will begin to welcome the time you set aside. Some days, your mind will be very active. Others, you will feel like you are sleeping. The Watcher will notice either/or, and all in between. There is no "not being able" to do this. You can't *not* be watching. The only thing that you can choose not to do is sit and close your eyes for a few minutes. But do it anyway; the juice is worth the squeeze.

CHAPTER 23

Spinning the Story

At the heart of every winter, there is a
quivering spring; and behind the veil of
each night there is a smiling dawn.

—Khalil Gibran

If you seek a new world, then you must
look with new eyes.

—Antoine de Saint-Exupery

In fairy tales, spinning a story means making it up as you go
along, and in fact, spinning your story, seeing story as moveable
rather than static, is one of the best ways to keep yourself in
the game of living the best story of your life. While you just
wrote your Old and New Stories, in every moment, we have the
opportunity to spin any story we are telling ourselves.

Recently, I read a study that explains when we retell stories, over 60 percent of the time we exaggerate, add on or omit
things. Most people change stories depending on who they are
talking to, they embellish to entertain and skip parts in order to

persuade. There's a trader at work who walked into his apartment two weeks ago, he's been married a year, and his wife was sitting there with her parents and a bodyguard saying there was an order of restraint against him. His story is that he's never been physically abusive. So who is telling the truth? The fact is, the stories we tell aren't necessarily factual, they are malleable, elastic, and we can tell them back to ourselves anyway we choose.

The trick is to only tell yourself stories that will help you move toward your New Story. When Rafael Nadal says that "no matter what the score, when I have just won a point, I know that I am winning," he's spinning his story to get to the win. He's telling himself a story about that one point that feels like a yes. Bill Russell, the basketball Hall of Famer, told the story that he loved playing against the best so that he could have a fuller, deeper experience. Thomas Edison spun the story when a reporter asked what it felt like to fail 1,000 times, and he replied, "I didn't fail 1,000 times. The light bulb was an invention with 1,000 steps." When hip surgery took me away from tennis for two years, rather than spin a tale of losing ground, I told myself I was resting so I would have the advantage of being well more well-rested than my opponents when I got back on the court. You might say, yes, but they are in shape or you are being unrealistic. That's not the story I'd choose to spin. Similarly, most people thought Carol was in denial when she got cancer. She went forward as if she wasn't going to die. Is that denial or is it spin? It's denial if you don't take care of yourself. It's a spin if the story gives you energy to take care of yourself. It's the story that worked for her; it kept her happy during the very end of her life.

Three years ago one of my longest and dearest friends from San Francisco found out he had Parkinson's disease and he immediately started to believe the bad stats around the disease; he spun a story about his health degenerating at an alarming rate. He started to fear the future. The truth is, no one knows that much about Parkinson's, so we can spin any tale we want. And he did. He spun a better story that has made his life, in some ways, better than before his diagnosis. He saw it as a motivator to get back on the treadmill that had been gathering dust. He reconnected with nature by going on daily hikes around Muir Beach. He took a new job that challenged him physically. He studied and practiced mindfulness as a way to keep his thoughts in the present. Three years later and the disease has barely progressed. Maybe coincidence, but he believes it is because he spun his story in a better way.

It's all a question of how you look at it.

I was coaching a 50-year-old tennis champion, who had been on the Senior Women's Davis Cup team ten times and had a bag of national championships. But she was challenged by a low self-image. Her game wasn't pretty, she didn't carry herself like a great athlete, she didn't wear trendy tennis clothes, she had thick glasses, and felt her wins weren't meaningful because she only won when others broke down against her. In short, she won a lot but felt like a loser. *My serve form is funny and the serve itself is wimpy. People just miss it because it's so slow. Everyone judges the way I serve. I win despite my serve.* We began to shift her self-image by flipping that story. *My serve is confusing for my opponents. They struggle to get the right timing on it. There are many serving styles and mine is unique to me just as Nadal's is to him. My serve gives me a chance to practice being nonreactive to other people's judgments and opinions about me.* Within two years she had won the World Championships with this bad serve and she had a new, healthy, feeling about herself.

Any story, in any moment can be flipped. In the fall of 2015, in a football game between two top-ranked rivals, University of Michigan was 10 seconds away from an upset win over Michigan State. With one play to make, the kicker fumbled and, in trying to recover the ball, he threw it into the hands of a State defender who ran it in for a touchdown. Game over, MSU.

I predicted his Old Story would go something like this: *"I am an idiot. I let myself choke in the biggest moment of my life. I disappointed my teammates, coaches, the University, the town and all the alumni. I can never show my face again in Ann Arbor. This error will define my life. I will never live this down. I need to go back to Australia. I will be a part of the list of screw-ups in sports like Bill Buckner, Chris Weber and Mickey Owens, the catcher that dropped the third strike and cost the Dodgers the World Series. My life is over."*

This story doesn't allow him to get out of this in a good way, it doesn't provide an exit from a life full of shame. In order to spin this story, we would have to ask him what kind of person he needs to be in order to survive this. What are this person's qualities? What would that person's story be around this experience? He may spin the story like this: *"This is an opportunity to learn how to forgive, to forgive myself for being imperfect, forgive others who judge me for my errors. It's a perfect time to practice acceptance, I accept results with dignity and class and accept myself even in dark moments. It gives me a chance to practice being nonreactive to what others think and say about me, to be courageous. I am a leader for my teammates in showing them how to get out of the quicksand. I am a model for climbing out of the darkness. I will apologize publicly and become a spokesman for owning up to errors, a model for the sports world."* When people ask him about it, he might say, "I had two choices. To believe in something that I could do to turn this into something good or to run away." Don't run away. There's always a way to spin the story. How do you spin your story? You ask yourself this simple question. In this scenario, where am I winning? Where's the positive? How can I grow from this? You feel frustrated with technology? You can flip that story to: *technology gives me a chance to practice patience, so I can become a more even person.* You're getting a divorce: *this allows me to find the partner I've always dreamed of.* You're late for lunch? *This allows me the chance to practice apologizing, which has always been difficult for me.*

Even a person wrongly convicted and in prison for over two decades can find a way to flip the story so it finds the yes as Nelson Mandela did. "A man who takes away another man's freedom is a prisoner of hatred," he has said. "He is locked behind the bars of prejudice and narrow-mindedness." He spun the story around so his jailers were imprisoned, and he was free.

Find the beauty of the spin.

SESSION TIP

The Big But: But what good does it do to make something up that I don't think is true? I am just kidding myself by spinning a bad story and pretending it is good.

Try This On For Size: Early on, I wrote that there are many different ways to take on adverse situations: thinking positively, changing your ringtone and being optimistic. If you want to move forward, you need to commit yourself to something that will remind you that the sun is always behind the clouds. It is; you can't deny it, it simply is. The fact of a good spun story is just as real as the badly spun story.

CHAPTER 24

Bring Your Angels, Not the Judges

The question isn't who is going to let me;
it's who is going to stop me.

—Ayn Rand

We judge ourselves by what we feel
capable of doing, while others judge us by
what we have already done.

—Henry Wadsworth Longfellow

Remember no one can make you feel
inferior without your consent.

—Eleanor Roosevelt

Ken was the son of one of the most famous jewelry designers
in the world. Because he wanted to make it on his own, he
started his own business. He was independent and had a good
dream, but he'd never worked hard at anything and had been

told over and over again he was an underachiever. I used to give him tennis lessons when he was 10, and when he heard through the grapevine that I was a change agent, he called me. His story was one filled with *lack of self- discipline, loss of focus, worry about competitors, inability to get things done, a short attention span, no exercise, fatigue from lack of sleep, and an unappreciative attitude toward what he had in his life: a good wife, a new baby, a supportive family. He said he was a pretty good golfer but even on the course he saw himself as an underachiever. He was a master of self-criticism.* His judge was a full-time tenant in his brain.

We worked on his New Story and got some good training plans going. Exercising, writing gratitudes, turning his desk chair away from the computer while talking to a client so he could focus. I wouldn't hear from him for days at a time. When I did, he would complain a lot about no changes. And then, after dropping off my radar for a whole month, he told me he didn't think he was a good client because he was only writing gratitudes a few times a week, and even though he was exercising daily, he wasn't doing it with enough intensity. And he complained that there were times that he wouldn't turn his chair away from the computer screen when talking to a client.

It turns out that he was actually practicing all the tools, and he was making progress, but his Old Story about being an underachiever distorted his view. Because he *believed* he was an underachiever, whatever he did was not enough. His judges kept up the constant refrain: *"If he just applied himself, he could do really well."* We packed those judges away in his Old Story. And we added the angels to his New Story. *My judges are deadbeat tenants that I have evicted from my brain. I carry my angels on my shoulders who applaud my every effort. I am a master of self-discipline, my middle name is focus, I love competition because it keeps me creating new and better systems. I apply myself and commit myself. I notice all the good things I do each day. I am a master at sticking with it. I surprise others by my ability to go above and beyond.* But the most powerful statement in there was this: *Who I am is enough.*

Once he had identified his judges, put them in his Old Story, and flipped the statements for his New Story, he found he jumped into his New Story full bore. He began to live his dreams: racing by the competition, completing every task he started, organizing his time to be incredibly productive. He became more grateful for his life, and even with three kids, he found more time to exercise. Now his energy is better than when he was 25. He has *become* the achiever.

Oh, and his golf has gotten better too.

Life is full of judges. Full of opportunities to integrate the criticism of others into our thought processes. Walt Disney was fired by a newspaper editor because "he lacked imagination and had no good ideas." He went bankrupt several times before he built Disneyland. The city of Anaheim rejected the proposal because they said it would attract riffraff.

Who among us is free of the judges that try to sabotage us? External judges from the past become the internal voices of "can't." That means we are often carrying around all the people who have influenced us by telling us we could have or should have been better as students, athletes, musicians.

Psychologist Eugene Sagan coined the term the Pathological Critic to describe the judges and let us know that it is a cultural phenomenon. Your judges will make you feel that you are the only one in the world with a shitty committee, but judges are something we all have in common. Sometimes you know just

where that committee started: the first grade teacher with ciga-
rette breath who told you that you'd never amount to anything,
the sibling who constantly berated you for being clumsy and
laughed at you in front of others, the art teacher who admon-
ished your drawing skills when you thought you were pretty
good. Who they are don't matter. It's your belief in what they said
that really matters. That belief needs to be overturned, upended
and dismissed. The way to that? Find what Abe Lincoln coined,
"Your better angels." Remember those people who believed in
you, who said you could do it, who congratulated you for a job
well done, even if you didn't get the A.

When competing I always had the feeling that my judges were
sitting on the fence, wearing black, looking down on me. Their
voices were filled with well-intentioned criticism. But their
words beat me down. They didn't help. One day I decided to
invite my angels to watch. They too were on the fence, but they
were wearing white gowns. They smiled down on me and their
voices reminded me of my effort, how good I was at getting up
after falling down, those things that I was doing well and why all
was good in the world. These were the voices I'd integrated from
every single person I had ever known who had believed in me.

The judges blame you for what went wrong, compare you
to others, set impossible standards and remind you of everything you failed at. They see your imperfections in the mirror
and convince you that others are uninterested, disappointed, or
repulsed by you. The judges use the words "always" and "never"
to describe your actions.

Let the voices of the angels drown out the vicious critic. The
angels see possibility, they tell you there is a next time, they take
life lightly, have a fabulous sense of humor, they are your guard-

ians and cheerleaders. The judges will dismiss the angels. They will say that your Sunday school teacher didn't count, and neither does your mother because it's her job to love you; they will say he only wants to marry you because he can't find someone else; they talk a lot about luck rather than skill. The angels are solid in their ability to see everything you have done before as a learning ladder for the next beautiful step; they know that mistakes are part of the game of life; angels love bad first drafts and bad hair days because they know without them, it's harder to feel the glory of the good times. The angels swing their feet; the judges skulk.

When you are hearing your judges, welcome your angels. Have them go to battle with the judges. If you need to, make a list—in your head or on paper—of all your accomplishments, of every time you have persisted and persevered, make a list of all the people who have loved and believed in you, even if one of them *is* your mother. At first the angels will neutralize the judges. One day soon, they will be your default voices. And your efforts will be rewarded.

SESSION TIP

The Big But: But I can't even remember any angels in my life. It seems like all my life people have been better at telling me what I'm *not* doing right rather than applauding me for what I do well.

Try This On For Size: The idea that you can only remember the negative is very common. It's actually a survival instinct in the brain. In olden times, when we had to fight to survive, we needed to focus on what *wasn't* right—the dangers in our environment—in order to make sure we weren't killed. This ancient part of our brain is still stimulated by negative thought. Remembering positive comments from people of influence in our lives may take time. You may need to sit down and really think back to times when you were complimented.

And when you do, don't dismiss them. Often we think thoughts like, "Well, she's my sister, she has to say that!" or, "That didn't really count; he said he loved my work, but then I didn't get the promotion after all." Be aware that dismissing the positive is just another way for the judges to have their say.

CHAPTER 25

Listening to the Door Slam

Talk of tomorrow is not one of the
conditions of the path.

—RUMI

Be here now. Be someplace else later.

—DAVID BADER

I have known a great many troubles, but
most of them never happened.

—MARK TWAIN

While playing effective tennis, the experience is mostly thought free. There's no time to think because you are in the midst of the action. But in between points the mind starts to interfere, missed opportunities and costly errors from the past start to creep into your thoughts. Future thoughts of worry about the score and the need to get this next point invade. The key to winning the game is often to find the way back to the state of no thought. That state of focus is a way of being, not doing. And you need to do something to get back to that state when you have fallen out of it. One of the best ways to find your way back to that quiet mental space is to listen.

I realized that, one day, when I was playing a match and my opponent was about to serve, I started to fall into an Old Story of allowing my judges to rule the game. "I have beaten him many times. I am at home on these courts. There is no reason for me to be in such a battle." I began chewing on the past and tripping into the future, I wasn't in the present. I had been in the space of noisy mind many times before and knew that entering the next point in this state of scattered thoughts was a good way to lose. I needed to enter the point in a state of presence, but how? "Everyone agrees it's important to live in the moment, but the problem is how?" asks Ellen Langer, a psychologist at Harvard University and author of *Mindfulness*.

Observing my breath had gotten old and wasn't dragging me back from the future or quieting my thoughts. And so, right before my opponent served, I tried something new. I closed my eyes and listened for the birds singing. The conversation in my mind was winning out. Maybe there weren't any birds around that day. But I kept listening, and then, sure enough I heard them. They had been there all the time but I hadn't heard them because my thoughts were so noisy. Shhhh. Listen. There they are! In that moment I found presence and I began to embody my New Story again. And what was so fantastic about it? I didn't have to take a yoga class to get there, I didn't have to meditate on a mountaintop, repeat a mantra, or read a book about it. By using all my attention to listen for something that was always there, I had returned to an instant state of now. Sometimes the birds aren't singing, or maybe, like my breath, I still had too much noise to hear them. There is something that takes even more quiet to hear and I would use that too. Listening to the wind moving through the leaves. Now that takes some serious listening. When I can hear the wind, I have definitely locked out the thoughts of past and future and I am back to where I want to be. Ready to start that next point.

We all know that living in the present is important. Living in the now is part of the yoga craze, and it's foundational in Buddhism, Taoism, and many Native American traditions. But we are mostly in monkey mind, where our thoughts careen from subject to subject. "We're living in a world that contributes in a major way to mental fragmentation, disintegration, distraction, decoherence," says Buddhist scholar B. Alan Wallace. "Ordinary thoughts course through our mind like a deafening waterfall," writes Jon Kabat-Zinn, the biomedical scientist who introduced meditation into mainstream medicine. Perhaps because of this, being in the now has become an industry. Eckhart Tolle's *Power of Now* sold over 2 million copies, articles are in the most traditional newspapers and on websites and countless studies have looked at the power of staying in the present. People have flooded workshops and retreats to learn how to listen to the birds to stay present.

Why? Because people who live in the present are said to have more self-confidence. They tend not to be as impulsive so they are less likely to overeat or drink. In short, they aren't trapped in their old stories. But does being present have to be so complicated? Do we have to stand on our heads, twist ourselves into pretzels, meditate for an hour a day? The happy answer is: no.

With a little bit of listening to what is waiting to be heard, moving into presence can be instantaneous.

Peter is head of southwest sales for a large software company and probably the best golfer in his club, but he'd never been able to win the club championship. "It starts this weekend," he told me. "And I need help. I heard you can do it." When we worked on his story, it turned out Peter had massive fears of losing, disappointing others, and being judged. So here is a guy who knows who he is, leads a great division, sells a massive amount of product to some of the biggest and brightest CEOs, but golf is his Achilles' heel.

When we looked at his story, it was clear he was putting too much attention on the future. Everything in his story—from losing to disappointing others had to do with what might happen, not what was happening.

We decided to write his New Story, one about playing for himself and knowing what he was capable of. In order to draw him back into the present when the Old Story of future tripping kicked in, we planned for him to do exactly what helped me that day on the court: listen. Not having much experience at listening with this kind of attention, he needed to practice. Remember, he only had one week until the club championship. Thankfully there are plenty of opportunities during each day to practice listening. He could start his day listening to his wife's shower running in the morning, then he could listen to the coffee percolating on the stove. Leaving the house he could listen to the screen door slam behind him. Another door slam when he gets into the car. Each of these listening experiences was practice to bring him instantly into a state of presence. With enough practice he would become a master of finding the quiet in his Old Story monkey mind. I wish

I could tell you that Peter won the championship later that week but he didn't. Runner up. But he did report back a few months later that he continued to listen to the doors slam and the birds sing and he has become more present at work and at home. No longer just doing the listening, he has become a being who lives in the now. I will bet on him winning the championship next year.

Psychologist Sonja Lyubomirsky, author of *The How of Happiness,* calls this "savoring." Be in the moment while you are eating a pastry, basking in the sun, or feeling the water run over you in the shower. Practice by choosing an activity that isn't usually worthy of our full attention: brushing your teeth, walking the stairs to the office, putting on your shirt in the morning. Once you practice in these arenas, you will better be able to move into the present when you need it most: a snag at work, a tough confrontation at home, or a competitive match.

Your Old Story voices are the past, so as soon as you can move to the present, you are out of your Old Story. Ellen Langer, who has been called, "the mother of mindfulness," also said that being in the present involves just the simple act of actively noticing things. She has actually never said you need meditation or yoga, though those are fine, too! "It could be playing the next bar in a scroll of music, or finding the next foothold if you're a rock climber, or turning the page if you're reading a good novel," says Mihaly Csikszentmihalyi, the psychologist who wrote *Flow: The Psychology of Optimal Experience.*

Beware. Living switching to the present moment instantaneously means abandoning old beliefs. In the present moment there is no judging, cherishing (old) opinions, or nurturing your discontent. After learning that listening to the birds was incredible for my tennis game, I learned later, when Carol was sick, that presence was also the best medicine. We lived by a line that we read in a greeting card, something that wiser people than us knew. *If you are thinking of the past or the future, you will lose out on the present.* Her sickness brought this to a place of reality for both of us and, as we listened to the doors slam and the thoughts of past and future were pushed out, we were left with the present.

And that is a great place to be.

SESSION TIP

The Big But: But this feels like minutia. I feel a tremendous amount of resistance when focusing on such a small thing. I'd like to make big changes, not these tiny time wasters.

Try This On For Size: To be able to hear the sounds that are always around us is actually your genius brain at work. From world-renowned concert pianists to scientists who changed the way we view the world, paying attention was one of the ways they arrived at brilliance. Whether it is the birds, the shower, the coffee percolating or the door slamming, this means squinting your brain and entering the space in your mind that is usually occupied by thoughts. The result is that you are left with huge focus and a presence that can lead to big ideas.

CHAPTER 26

Nap Time and Other Necessary Luxuries

Every now and then go away, have a little
relaxation, for when you come back to
your work your judgment will be surer.

—LEONARDO DA VINCI

Take rest; a field that has rested gives a
bountiful crop.

—OVID, ROMAN POET

Sleep is the best meditation.

—THE DALAI LAMA

Albert Einstein is said to have gotten ten hours of sleep a night as well as daytime naps. After Arianna Huffington collapsed from exhaustion in 2007, she made rest one of the primary themes of her recent book, *Thrive*, and now has nap rooms at the Huff Post offices. Warren Buffett insists sleep is better than extra profits.

Be aware that when you are on your journey to a new and better version of yourself, to being your New Story, it is okay, actually crucial, to stop and take a break. Every great religion including Buddhism, Judaism, Christianity, Islam, Bahia, and Wiccan (among others) teach the importance of setting aside time to rest. Andre Agassi, when asked what it was like to try to improve every day, said, "it is exhausting." This may be our biggest problem. Sometimes we try too hard. Effortless effort can be your work for today. Put your feet up, let a new energy take over. The change is happening. You have put things into gear.

Of course, this may be easier said than done, rest is probably the most difficult activity high functioning people engage in. The Centers for Disease Control recently called lack of sleep a public health problem. We are a "doing" culture. Just that question, "What do you do?" seems to be a judgment call on who you are as a person.

And if you are someone who has big goals and wants to reach huge horizons, rest can seem like a waste of time. It's not. Tired people tend to be less productive at work. Rest helps you think more clearly, gives you quicker reflexes, and gives you better focus. Rest balances our molecular and energetic bodies as well as our brain function and mood. Ongoing sleep deficiency is linked to an increased risk of heart disease, kidney disease, high blood pressure, diabetes, and stroke.

Most importantly, when you are tired it can be really hard to work toward your New Story. A high powered New York attorney, Larry, was living an Old Story: *My life is in a terrible state. I feel worthless. I am overweight, out of shape, depressed.* As we got to work, he began to move toward his New Story: *I search for the joyful moments in my days. I identify those ways that I help others.*

I treat my body with respect, fueling it with only the best food. I am grateful for my life. (Remember, you can write any New Story you want, so you might as well right a good one.) He used the tools of optimism and talking to himself positively. He'd loved riding a bike as a kid, but his Old Story included feeling like he was supposed to give to others and that he was unworthy of giving to himself. After writing his New Story, though, and practicing it, he bought an expensive road bike and he started to cruise around his neighborhood.

His body began to change. He began to make long weekend rides for charity and this helped him value himself. He was giving to the world in a way that he never had. He became a leader and started a foundation that, through biking, raised money for under-privileged children. Unfortunately, things got tough at home. He and his wife were not on the same page. They had a severely disabled daughter, and they had not planned well for the inevitability of having to find a place for her as she hit her teens. Larry started to sink. He stopped exercising. He no longer wrote his gratitudes. He stopped reaching out to others. He stopped riding.

And then something happened that seemed like a slap in the face, but was actually the best thing for him: the law firm he worked for ordered him to take a sabbatical to get his life in order. He needed to regain his focus and his commitment to the firm.

A rest was exactly what he needed. In the six months away, he began to heal himself. Writing new and better stories of who he would be. He wrote his gratitudes. He got back to the gym. He got back on the bike, he began to live his New Story again. Larry lets us know two really important things: you can always get back on the bike or back to your New Story and sometimes in order to do that, you need rest.

If you have a hard time resting, how do you convince your spinning mind that rest is the best thing for it? Your mind is often afraid to rest because of the Old Story of not having accomplished enough. Your mind is often looking back at where you were and comparing it to where you are now. You can look back ten years, then five. You can look back at last year at this time and notice not only how much you have accomplished, but how much you have grown. What have you accomplished this month? Before you go to bed or take a night off, list all that you have accomplished that day.

Stop and cruise for a while. And remember even as you sleep, watch a movie, ski down a mountain you are changing. Your body is balancing and repairing, your subconscious is working out unresolved dilemmas, your brain is figuring out that problem you left on your desk. Change happens while you sleep. Rest.

SESSION TIP

The Big But: But there isn't enough time in the day for me to get my work done, commute, get home to see the kids, spend time with my wife, exercise, and take a shower. Now you want me to rest?

Try This On For Size: Whoa, slow down a moment. Did you ever try to dig a hole on the beach? There is no end; there is always more sand in the hole. So it is with life. You can stay up 24 hours a day and still not have enough time.

Stop fighting that losing battle. Put aside a few minutes in your day to rest your mind and body. You will be able to get more done afterward.

CHAPTER 27

Celebrate Your Successes/ Shrink Your Failures

All too often, our natural talents go untapped. From the cradle to the cubicle, we devote more time to fixing our shortcomings than to developing our strengths.

—Tom Rath

Our ultimate freedom is the right and power to decide how anything outside ourselves affects us.

—Stephen Covey

After a game I often ask a player, "How did you do?" Typically, if they lost, and often when they won, they will list all the bad things they did. Missed shots. Stupid choices. Leads lost.

What they should and could have done better. I always follow up with "What did you do well? After all you played for nearly two hours. Is there nothing you did well?" "No, I stumbled. I got tired. I was fearful. I hit three double faults." Old Stories, rather than new ones.

Because they often struggle to come up with an answer about what they did right, I lead them there by breaking down their game. *Did you fight off negative thoughts? How did you do on your toss? Did you take your time? How did you move? Did you give good effort? Did you avoid making excuses?* These are their successes. I encourage the player to list everything they did well; these are the moments when they were living out their New Stories. *"I fought hard. When I was down, I kept pushing. I stayed positive. I worked to find a solution. I didn't quit. I smiled and told an optimistic story. I patted myself on the back and kept talking positively to myself. I was a good loser who made no excuses."* Whenever you exercise any of your New Story—celebrate. Shrink the Old Story. Fight the default way of thinking that you didn't do this or that.

It is our way to find the negatives. New research in neuroscience has shown that we're wired to remember the negative more than positive. The amygdala, the part of the brain that perceives negative activity is there to anticipate danger, and protect us. For this reason, the brain is, as neuroscientist Rick Hanson says, "like Velcro^R for negative experiences and Teflon™ for positive ones."

Perhaps for the simple reason that it's our default reaction to focus on the negative, we've been taught to think that our weaknesses and mistakes define us. We think by focusing on what is wrong, we will become better. But what we focus on grows. In fact, the more they talk about what they did "wrong," the more they do "wrong." Listing the failures rarely changes a thing.

I work with a figure skater whose goal is to become a member of Team USA. Recently, she called to tell me she's been fighting a binge eating disorder. Her story is this: *I'm living at home, and I'm struggling with my dad who is trying to fix me when I need to fix myself. I'm disappointed with what I am losing out on, I'm embarrassed and ashamed.* I told her, "I'm here for you." Because a part of her original Old Story was *"I don't like it when people felt sorry for me when I'm not competing well,"* I skipped the sympathy response and congratulated her, saying, "You just did a courageous thing by letting me know and reaching out to me. It shows how amazing you are. You didn't run away."

But she fought the success. "I did run," she said. "For months, I knew you could help me, but I didn't tell you." At a time when she most needed to celebrate a success she was building up a failure.

And now she wished she'd told me earlier because her therapist told her it would take a year to get healthy. That thought had rooted in her mind and she knew that I might have had a different angle.

She was right about that. "Really? One whole year? Is that written somewhere? Sounds like data shmata to me."

"Well, that's what the therapist said."

In order to begin to celebrate her successes I told her, "This therapist doesn't know you. Do they know that you run toward adversity rather than being afraid of it? That you are highly competitive? That you can move into a New Story in three months? That you look for every minute of the day to practice it? Hey, look, how about a New Story? *You are a champion, you come through all kinds of adversity as a skater and this is just another challenge.*" By celebrating her past successes, she began to feel strong enough to write a New Story. Fifteen minutes after we got off the phone, she had emailed me her New Story. *I feel no shame. I just stepped into a hole and I've gotten out of much deeper holes in my life.* Her story included speaking to her friends who support her. Tolerating her own imperfections. No future tripping. In the days to come, in order to keep her moving toward the New Story, we talked about all of her past successes, and how past successes meant that she was strong enough to succeed in this capacity. *My focus is deep and enduring. I always find the way. No one practices as much as me. I am technically among the most sound. I mentor younger skaters coming up through the ranks. I am a role model for success.*

Knowing how victorious she has been in developing the skill of letting go of counterproductive thoughts in other situations has allowed her to observe the thoughts that occur in her mind when her dad talks about fixing her. She's able to be nonreactive. She's able to take one step at a time. By celebrating her successes, she is able to continuously think, "I can" rather than "I can't." By bringing her angels with her every day, she continued to do the work of her New Story, and now she is back on the ice. And she has proved to the therapist that other people's stories don't apply to her.

Whether in the schools, at work, on the court, within our families, or in the therapist's office, we're always being asked: What is wrong with you? How can we fix you? When I ask a trader how the day was, he often says, "I blew it, I was too early or late on that trade. I lost money." So I ask, "What was *good* in your day. Nothing? You were at work all day. Did you make any good decisions? Did you put in any good trades? Did you make effort? Did you fight against resistance? Did you give a dollar to the homeless man on the corner?"

If we focus on improving our weaknesses, we may get them to be functional. That is okay and worth some effort. But if we celebrate our strengths we can take them from very good to extraordinary.

SESSION TIP

The Big But: But if I shrink my failures, how will I ever manage to fix what needs to be fixed in my life? I believe that my failures need some attention so that I don't repeat past mistakes.

Try This On For Size: True, our failures need attention, but only insofar as we can balance them with what we are doing right. Remember that what you focus on, grows. Focus on your failures, and you will find yourself failing more. Focus on your successes, and you will find you succeed at a far greater rate. Once you know where your strengths and your talents lies, you can move from that vantage point, and the failures will begin to fall away.

CHAPTER 28

Love Your Triggers

When you blame and criticize others, you
are avoiding some truth about yourself.

—Deepak Chopra

It took Iraqi veteran, Geoffrey Miller four years to be able to drive over manhole covers, and he still feels a cold sweat every time. When he was at war, manholes were perfect places for the Iraqis to hide IEDs (improvised explosive devices). Now that the manhole cover has become a threat, it feels nearly impossible to Jeff to decondition his brain from reacting. Even though a manhole in Cleveland probably wouldn't be housing an IED, Geoffrey's brain doesn't know it, and before therapy, he would have the reaction of someone about to face critical danger. This is a trigger.

Triggers are recognizable by an extreme reaction that's out of proportion to the situation. When Geoffrey sees a manhole, he is reliving an old, really terrifying story. This clinical notion of triggering dates back to World War I, when psychologists started to recognize that veterans were getting triggered by something that resembled their original trauma. Anticipating triggers can be difficult because they are notoriously unpredictable, but once triggered, you can find yourself right back in your Old Story. They often stem from something traumatic or upsetting that happened in childhood. Someone makes a comment or does something and suddenly an emotional gun has gone off inside you, and you are sent reeling back into your Old Story. So, how are you expected to love that? Actually, when seen in the right light, triggers can be your fast track to your New Story.

When I was first developing my tennis game, I used to hit a terrible shot when someone attacked my backhand, which was my weaker shot. I'd freak out and try to blast it, something I had no skill at. Or I would react defensively and lob weakly. Neither of these reactions was effective. Then a wise coach who understood more than just forehands and backhands asked me, "What do you do when someone attacks you in life?" I said, "I get defensive or attack back." Wisely he told me, "Well, this isn't life. In tennis it is fair play to come after your backhand. This is not like life. Out here, people do what they need to do to win."

He was right. On the court, the other player was trying to trigger me. In life, people often have no idea they are triggering you, and once you realize that, it's easier to see the trigger as a gift. But because triggers are uncomfortable, they often lead to blaming and we miss the gift.

Early in our relationship, Jo Ann and I were going to dinner in the city. Most of the parking areas were crazy expensive, and I finally found one that was $30 bucks for a couple of hours. When we were ready to drive home, the parking attendant handed me a ticket for $40 because we were leaving after 10 PM. The small print tripped me up. I started yelling at the parking guy, "This is unfair, the sign says $30 and the ticket says $40, I'm going to take a picture of the sign and send it to the commissioner" and "I'm not giving you a tip" . . . That's not my normal way of behaving, especially in front of a woman I wanted to be with for the rest of my life, but this trigger of being ripped off was passed down to me from my mom, and I just had at it.

As I was driving home, I started thinking about that parking guy. He was working late on a weekend night, he was just doing his job, it wasn't his fault the ticket came out to $40 instead of $30. I had been triggered by an Old Story. Instead of blaming him, I began to feel compassion toward him, and as my outlook changed, I came to a realization. This incident with the parking attendant was a gift, a golden opportunity: he had shown me where I was still stuck, where I was still living an Old Story. A story that wasn't working for me. Once I knew I was still stuck in an old belief system around being ripped off, I could begin to write a New Story about it. But if I got stuck in blame (that guy is wrong), I never would have had the opportunity to find a better story.

This is easier if it's the parking guy, harder if it's someone you know. Recently, a client, Lindsay, was away for a girls' weekend and had taken it upon herself to buy all the food and to do the cooking. One of the other girls, a friend of hers who never cooks, said something judgmental about her cooking. Lindsay's emotional temperature went through the roof. *How dare she say something about my cooking, she never even pitches in and now she's complaining about what I prepared? How could she?* Lindsay is a high-powered businesswoman who started with very little. She'd just gotten out of an abusive relationship when she started her business, and she had to do absolutely everything on her own with no help from a spouse or family. She can get easily triggered by people who sit on the sidelines, criticizing others, while not lifting a finger themselves.

This is a challenging trigger because Lindsay has a point. If it's a girl's weekend away, it works best when everyone is participating. So, Lindsay justified her trigger and when she felt calmer took her friend aside and said, *Listen honey, you said something about how I cooked and it really bothered me. Maybe you could work on chipping in more and being grateful that I am cooking rather than being judgmental.*

In fact, what she was doing here was working on the other person rather than working on herself. Most of us know about the guy at the bookstore who went to the self-help section. Under the section: *How to change your spouse* every book was sold out. But under the section: *How to change yourself,* there was an abundance of stock on the shelves. It's easier to get someone to change a little bit, so that *we* don't get triggered in the same way, but if the other person makes an adjustment and no longer does that particular thing, then we have not grown. And when the trigger comes up again, we still have to deal with it. When we blame someone else, we actually give them the power over our happiness.

How do you catch a trigger and avoid flying off the handle? Sometimes you can't, the reaction is so strong you're already yelling before you have a chance to catch it. Other times, you don't want to catch it because you feel like crying, screaming, you feel punched in the gut, you feel like you are right no matter what and you have to prove it, immediately.

But on your best days you catch it by noticing. Notice if you are having an extreme reaction to something that isn't a way you normally react. Or want to react. Ask yourself, is this a trigger? With practice you will spot a trigger and turn it into a gift.

Carlos Castaneda wrote of petty tyrants, people who make us feel small and unimportant. If we are to become who we want to become, we must fight these tyrants with the one thing that will work: we must love them. Love reduces them to a state of no power over us. Why do we love them? Because they show us the places in our lives where we feel small and unimportant, so we can write a New Story about these places and begin to move forward.

Often we are triggered by qualities in others we want to change in ourselves: "complains a lot" "stays stuck in a dead-end job or marriage" "talks about doing X but never does anything about it." Whatever the trigger, as soon as you catch it, you can say a quick *thank you!* for the gift of knowing where you are stuck, and then write an Old Story about that trigger, and write a New Story soon afterward. If I am triggered by another's impatience, my New Story should include patience. If I am offended by grandiosity, I'm probably insecure and trying to hide it. My New Story needs to include confidence.

Skeptics may argue that altering your thinking doesn't change the problem, just your perception of it, but that's the magic of it. Whatever the present moment contains, accept it as if you had chosen it. Always work with it, not against it. Make it your friend and ally, not your enemy. This will miraculously transform your whole life. This is higher awareness, and it's often the prelude to a solution. Accept, love, only then, act.

SESSION TIP

The Big But: But it's hard to love your triggers when you are mad as hell at someone or some situation. I feel pretty myopic when I am triggered.

Try This On For Size: You can't always love your trigger when you are in it. That's okay. It's in the aftermath that change happens.

Once you realize that you were, indeed, in the middle of a trigger, you can figure out what happened. A trigger is always a bad story, so writing out that old story, or even just identifying it in thought, gets you on your way to a new story, and in the end, a lot less triggering.

CHAPTER 29

Incinerating the Past

Finish each day and be done with it. You
have done what you could.

—RALPH WALDO EMERSON

I have a friend who went back to school for her bachelor's degree
when she was in her thirties. She was a single mom with four
kids and didn't have enough money, so she took out a student
loan. That was more than 20 years ago and every year she didn't
pay, her interest rates went up. If she put it off, they still got to
raise the rates. Then they sold her loan to a collection agency,
and they started raising the rates year after year. Her loan was
$30,000, now it's up to $70,000.

Her Old Story was one of money issues and never feeling on
top of things. Her New Story was that she made good decisions with money and that she didn't accumulate debt. "But,"
she said. "If I really want to be that New Story, first I have to get
rid of this debt."

"Actually you can start now," I told her. "Today you *do* make good decisions, today you are not accumulating debt. Why let a decision you made a long time ago define you?"

Incinerating the Past and leaving no traces is a Zen concept that is the flip side of future tripping. No gain exists in either time zone. And forgetting is actually a powerful, spiritual concept. It goes against a lot of our learning. We have been taught to "learn from your past mistakes." but when you dwell on the past you can defeat yourself with regret, blame, or missed chances. It's easy to imprison yourself with rules from the past. *I got hurt before, I will get hurt now.* Living by forgetting is paradoxically how we won't make the same mistakes going forward.

In order for your New Story to work, the Old Story has to *stay* in the past and that can be a mind blow for us because we've been told that dissecting our past can lead to fewer mistakes and triggers in the future. If the Old Story voice is troubling you, bring out your New Story voice and, for the moment, let it win the argument. These are your voices and you can, just for now, choose which wins. But for sure, while you *are* in the game, at the negotiation table, having the relationship chat, it's important to make note of those things that are creeping up from the past, and stay in the now, knowing you will deal with the past later. The past can be a good excuse for us not living our New Stories. Keep the good memories but incinerate the past that is keeping you from moving forward.

Don't let something that is no longer happening be the bad fruit that is ruining the whole vine.

SESSION TIP

The Big But: But shouldn't we learn from the past? If I forget about the past, won't I keep making the same mistakes over and over again?

Try This On For Size: There are times to look at the past. These are the non-emotional moments where you can analyze what is going on in your Old Story/New Story mind and create a brand New Story moving forward (see the "Love Your Triggers" Session Tip). In order to write an old story, we have to go into the past. But there are times when incinerating the past is necessary in order to give ourselves the chance to start over. Think of times you've been the new kid on the block, new school, new job, new neighborhood. Scary? Yes! But it also gives you a beautiful chance to reinvent yourself.

CHAPTER 30

Mental Training 101

We either make ourselves miserable, or
we make ourselves happy. The amount of
work is the same.

— CARLOS CASTANEDA

Every thought is a seed. If you plant crab
apples, don't count on harvesting golden
delicious.

— BILL MEYER

Kind words can be short and easy to
speak, but their echoes are truly endless.

— MOTHER TERESA

Every time you say something negative to yourself, it's a
footprint in the brain. Sooner or later, with enough repeated
steps, there is going to be a path and then a rut. The rut will
continue to deepen until you become conscious and pay attention
to where you are walking. Once you gain an awareness of your

moment-to-moment thoughts and the emotions and beliefs that follow, you begin to get the space to be able to speak positively to yourself. You can teach an old dog new tricks, provided you are willing to take the dog walking down a new path.

It's difficult to move toward our new stories if we are constantly talking badly to ourselves. The trick to self-talk is to be a friend to yourself. We are so often our worst critic, but when we become friends with ourselves, we can give ourselves the same encouragement we might give to a buddy when he calls on the phone with a problem. In one study at the University of Michigan, researchers told participants they had to prepare a speech to give to a panel of judges about their qualifications in order to get the job of their dreams. Half the participants were told to talk themselves through their own anxiety by using the "I" pronoun as in: "I shouldn't be nervous. The other half were told to address themselves by using their name or the second person, such as, "don't be nervous"; or "Bob, don't be nervous." Afterward, the second group reported less shame than the ones who used "I." The judges found the performances of those using "you" to be more confident, less nervous, and more persuasive.

In Dr. Masaru Emoto's book, *The Hidden Messages of Water,* first published in Japan with over 400,000 copies sold, he demonstrated how our thoughts and feelings affect physical reality. By exposing some frozen water to encouraging, positive words, the water formed brilliant, complex, and colorful patterns. Alternatively when the water was exposed to negative words, it formed incomplete, asymmetrical patterns with dull colors, giving us an interesting experiment that shows not only do our actions respond to positive self-talk, but we could be moving toward a healthier physical body as well.

Charles is a hedge fund trader. He is big, a former football player, a gentle bear. When he hugs me I check for broken ribs. He is a little scary-looking when he wears his sleeveless leather vest and shows up on his Harley-Davidson. When we met, I liked him immediately. He seemed like a good man, caring, generous, loyal.

He sees the world through a negative lens. *I'm not as smart as other guys in the office. I am too scared to put a position on. I never make enough money. I am going to get fired. I can't control my frustration. I feel unhealthy. I don't contribute enough to the firm. I can't stay focused. I feel like I am falling apart.* He's got an autistic son, and it's difficult for him. *I'm not sure that I am making the right decisions for his future.*

We went to work on Charles's story. He wanted to be more confident at work, to practice patience when it came to his temper; he wanted to be a better father, to become one of those men people admire for steadfastness and balance. To deal with the Old Story that he was falling apart, I had him write down three positive things for every negative comment he said about himself. *I got up this morning and pushed myself to go to the gym. I was pissed at a driver who cut me off but I fought off sitting on my horn. I said good morning to someone in the office who had ignored me yesterday. I can't make money* was followed by *I am a good father. I stopped by my neighbor's house to see how she was doing after I heard that her sister had a stroke. I cut back some overgrown trees.* Over time it became more natural for Charles to think to himself more positively. It didn't need to be an antidote to negative thoughts, he just started to think more positively about the good that he did and the good in his life.

He had become overweight in his depressed, negative, "terrible state." But he started to exercise daily and found he could lose himself there and enter a state of presence. As he improved he felt better about himself. At work he made adjustments and started to face his fears. He began to recognize his value at work. Maybe he would not make as much money as the best, but he became a valuable mentor to some of the younger, less experienced traders.

He also helped build deep relationships with the big banks the firm would need to partner with when companies were going public. He was able to generate good income from that part of the business. As his confidence started to grow, he even started trading a little more. He made a plan to put on a position each morning, as practice, so that he would build courage. Little by little he made progress. For a while, he was the biggest producer in the firm. By speaking positively to himself, he discovered a new world of hope, of possibilities that, before, he was unwilling to allow himself to even dream about. He found that by speaking positively to himself, he was able to live his New Story. Because, in essence, the Old Story is your negative self-talk. The New Story is your positive self-talk.

In short, be kind and supportive to yourself and you will be moving toward your New Story faster. Write a list of words like exceptional, incredible, outstanding, extraordinary, special, ultimate, master, unbeatable. Use these words to describe your life to your friends, colleagues, family. Be outrageous. These words are deposits into your personal bank account that will offset the default way we tend to view and talk about ourselves.

SESSION TIP

The Big But: But I hate when people tell me to "think positively." It sounds so easy, and yet when I am in the midst of something tough, how can I just turn off what's actually happen and think positively instead? It's unrealistic!

Try This On For Size: Think of negative thoughts as a sabateur that wants to sabotage everything you are working toward and all your success. This saboteur is very sneaky and tends to creep around, trying to catch us in its traps.

Do you see how even this question includes negative thinking? The key isn't to push the negative thoughts aside. It is to recognize that they are there and try to find the positive thoughts that are available to you in that moment. Eventually the saboteur will give up and sneak away.

CHAPTER 31

Getting to Carnegie Hall

We are what we repeatedly do. Excellence, then, is not an act but a habit.

—ARISTOTLE

Even if you're on the right track, you'll get run over if you just sit there.

—WILL ROGERS

. . . eventually, as you gradually build up the positive practices, the negative behaviors are automatically diminished.

—HIS HOLINESS THE DALAI LAMA

Marjorie is an incredible woman, a venture capitalist who managed a 60-hour work week. She felt she had very little time with her three kids, and not much connection with her husband. Their lives were so chaotic, she felt disengaged from her community. Her idea involved huge change: moving to their vacation home in the mountains of Vermont, where she would be engaged and feel part of a larger community.

Since she couldn't move to Vermont overnight, I suggested practicing being engaged right here in Manhattan.

"But how?" she asked me, looking at her New Story rather mournfully. "Practice engaging with everyone you see," I told her. "Make eye contact, say hello, make a connection, be in the present, really see people, rather than rushing by to the next thing."

The next day she told me that she was standing in line at Starbucks for her daily coffee fix, and she noticed that no one was looking at the baristas. Everyone was looking at or talking on their cell phones, including her. So, when she went up to the counter, she looked right at the name tag and then looked up at the barista. "Good morning, Rachel," she said. And then she smiled wide and ordered her coffee. For Marjorie, this was a huge change.

"Bob," she told me, "the jolt I got from engaging with a stranger in that way gave me a bigger jolt than the caffeine from my coffee. I love it!"

And she did it every day. It became her practice.

Within no time, the practice had grown. She was seeing the mornings when the kids were getting ready for school as the sweetest moments in the day. She looked at them, listened to them, engaged with them. And she was building a community around her by smiling, saying hello, taking a few minutes to notice who was in her immediate world. And she never had to move to Vermont.

Living your New Story takes practice. Change takes practice. Sigmund Freud was booed from the podium when he first presented his ideas to the scientific community of Europe. He returned to his office and kept writing. Robert Sternberg got a C in his first college introductory psychology class. His teacher told him, "there was a famous Sternberg in psychology and it's obvious there won't be another." Three years later Sternberg graduated with honors from Stanford University with exceptional distinction in psychology, summa cum laude, and Phi Beta Kappa. He has since become president of the American Psychological Association. Charles Darwin was told by his father, "You care for nothing but shooting, dogs, and rat catching." In his autobiography, Darwin wrote, "I was considered by all my masters and my father, a very ordinary boy, rather below the common standard of intellect." What is the difference between those who are considered failures and fail and those who succeed? It's practice, whether in psychology or science, in building community or thinking positively, practice is what makes musicians play beautifully, athletes score goals, orators move a crowd, and businessmen close the deal. The truth is, no matter how good you are, you go through tough periods. Michael Jordan would miss his first eight shots of the game, but he'd have no difficulty taking the ninth. Rookies, though, if they miss two in a row, get scared and tend to freeze.

There is no shortage of tips about how to improve your life, your work, your forehand, or your putting, your relationships. But none of these tips: be positive, observe your breath, exercise, make priority lists, focus, relax, really work unless you practice them. A lot. And then, with enough practice, these tips fold into your being. Into who you are. And then, they are no longer tips to try to remember and do. They are you.

As cognitive scientist Daniel Willingham says, "It is difficult to overstate the value of practice. And what's necessary is sustained practice. Practicing beyond the point of mastery is necessary to meet your goals and become an expert." We tend to think practice means several hours a day, it takes time, endurance, a ton of energy. In fact practice can be something simple that takes only a few moments out of a busy schedule, with big results.

Will has been at a junior trader for about 2 1/2 years. He was a rookie out of college when he first arrived, a big, athletic, modest person who knows the ropes of high-level competition. These firms put applicants through a rigorous interview with all the partners and consultants having an opinion. They hire for success. So Will had their confidence on the day they asked him to join the fund. As with many who get hired, his expectations were for success.

The first year he got training on the model by sitting next to a big producer. In order to learn, he watched him closely. Finally, early this year, he got his break. He was moved into his own seat with his own book. That means he would be trading the firm's dollars and would make money based on his success investing. But after seven months, he was struggling. He hadn't gotten feedback from his performance that would suggest future success. He was like a great minor league pitcher who, when brought up to the majors has a learning curve. In the big stadium, sharing a dugout with some of the stars, he was going up against big reputations, and he felt like he was letting the team down when the game was on the line. The better story was that he was learning, rapidly, how to make it in the majors. Maybe he wouldn't get that many wins this year. Maybe he would strike out a lot. That was the cost of learning.

Will wanted to continue focusing on the technical aspects of trading. He didn't trust that these skills would develop over time, as he would learn to see more with more experience.

So, we decided to practice something that would help him begin to work on what was beneath his work story: worried thinking manifesting as stress. Sometimes a client will tell me they are feeling stressed, and they say, *It's weird because I meditated this morning and I went to a yoga class this week.* That's great, but what can you do about the stress right *now*? That's the practice, being able to do something every time you get stressed. Why wait? So, every time Will felt stressed, he also took one deep breath. Just one was fine, but it was the fact that he did it *every* time that mattered.

We set a time every hour to separate for just two minutes to observe his breathing. It took him down a notch in a good way. He started doing it frequently throughout the day even when he didn't think he needed it. You don't just go to the gym when you think you need it, right? You don't tell your fiancé that you love her just because you need to, right?

After several weeks of staying committed to this practice, Will was able to identify a lot of what was going on inside him and felt ready to write his Old Story: *I don't trust myself. I think others know more than me. I am frustrated. I am letting others down. I can't let go of the past. I beat myself up. I compare myself to theirs. I question my dream of working in finance. I am fearful. I let work results affect my mood and my life. I doubt myself. I am scared. I am running out of time.*

That's a rough Old Story. The good news is that negative thoughts, deficit emotions, lack of self-belief, and shaky focus are all changeable; they aren't truths. They're just thoughts that we repeat to ourselves, and because Will had proven to himself that he was good at practicing a simple task of observing breath, he knew that he could practice his New Story: *I trust myself. I belong in the trading room as much as anyone else. I am in my learning curve and I am honing my skills daily. I learn from those who have more experience than me. I am accepting of my inability to be perfect. I am judgment free.*

I knew all it would take was a little practice, and that his New Story was his for the taking.

What do you think might happen if you practiced just one thing a little bit every day? Observing your breath, saying thank you, speaking warmly to your mail carrier.

A better story? A light in the darkness on the path?

SESSION TIP

The Big But: But having to practice, practice, practice makes me feel like I'm a workhorse. Can't I ever just get it? Isn't it possible that sometimes it comes easily, and you don't have to do the daily slog of practicing?

Try This On For Size: The trick to practicing is to Redefine Winning (Chapter 17) in the practicing. You want to get to the point where practicing the new story is just as fun as getting to the "end game," where you are actually living it. So, if a musician loves playing the violin, Carnegie Hall is just a byproduct of all those days and nights he got to spend with his instrument and practicing, practicing, practicing. If you feel like your New Story is a slog, you might have to write a new one! Getting there should be just as much fun as actually "achieving" it.

CHAPTER 32

Fake It 'Til You Make It

Be brave. Even if you're not, pretend to be. No one can tell the difference.

—JACKSON BROWNE

Act on the outside the way you want to feel on the inside.

—TRACY McMILLAN

Back in 2009, Stephanie L. Stolz of Missouri Western University conducted an interesting study where she researched what served as negative and positive reinforcements for mundane tasks. She discovered what we have always suspected: confidence has a large effect on performance. Fake it 'til you make it is actually one of the easiest ways you can manufacture confidence because if you act one way, the brain automatically begins to send signals that you *are* in fact that way.

The emotional receptors fire a New Story for you, and before you know it, you *are* that person.

One year I was watching Boris Becker and Stefan Edberg play a really close match in the finals at Wimbledon. When Edberg won, Becker stepped over the net and hugged him. I thought to myself, *I want that. I want to feel really happy for the other person when I'm in defeat.* They'd just played four hours of pretty equal tennis; it just so happens Edberg won, so why not feel good about my playing even if I didn't get match point? Why not be happy for the other person? I never feel as good about my own playing when my opponent isn't playing well, so I might as well congratulate him.

I'd had happiness as a winner, but I wanted to experience the feeling even when I was the loser. I started to go to work on it. Throughout that year, I would invent active energy around it. I may not have felt the joy I wanted to feel when I was defeated, but I would *act* like I did, and I would say complimentary things to the other person anyway. Acting on the outside, like I might not have felt on the inside.

Then one day, I was playing match point against someone I really respected, and suddenly some guy walked onto the court to say he'd reserved it. I was about to serve to win the match and this was so disrupting that I double faulted, and my opponent wound up winning the match.

In the locker room I told my opponent it was a great match, and that he'd played really well. It took some effort but it also felt really good. This was progress toward a New Story of who I aspired to be. He was amazed, and told me how mad he would have gotten if he had been serving and some guy walked over, demanding his court time.

Not long afterward I went to Santa Barbara to defend the national championships with the intent of acting like a champion, win or lose. I made it to the semi-finals and wound up losing. And when I said to the guy, "I'm so excited for you, for being in the finals," I finally really felt genuine about it. It was authentic, real. He later told me he won the finals in part because of seeing what I was like after losing. Losing can still be winning.

Fake it 'til you make it, placebo effect, the self-fulfilling prophecy, acting on the outside like you want to feel on the inside is not new, but it *can* be the missing ingredient when we feel so far from our New Story, we feel we'll never get there.

I was working with an incredible guy who had beautiful kids and a lot of people who admired him in his field. But he was always complaining that he wasn't doing better. For fifteen years, he'd hired amazing teachers, from a Zen meditator he flew in from Australia, to high-level coaches like myself, but he never really practiced the skills he was taught. "Listen," I finally said. "Let's get to work on this stuff."

And he finally admitted, "I'm not sure if I can do it."

His problem was that he was expecting to change just from coaches, teachers, and trainers talking to him. He wasn't actually doing anything. So, we decided to go to work on his Old Story. One of his biggest stumbling blocks was patience. He was a Type A guy. He ate fast, talked fast, traded fast. He was impatient with his employees, his kids, his friends, the barista at the corner shop, and the chef at the sushi bar. He liked high-energy activities and he had a hard time staying with the same girlfriend, never mind trying out some of the tools that would get him to close the gap from the old to the New Story. "But I've never been patient," he told me when I pointed out what a big part of the Old Story it was. "How the hell am I going to do it now?"

"Fake it," I told him. "This is your opportunity to practice this in all kinds of little ways, so if someone crosses you, if a waiter or waitress brings you the wrong food, and you are feeling intolerant, act differently on the outside. Rather than showing your impatience and saying something like "I can't believe you brought me this," smile at them say, "Gee, that wasn't quite what I wanted, can you change this?" Fake it for this one time. It will be a start. Kaizen. One step at a time.

So every day, he pretended he was a patient guy. Waiting for the elevator at work had been excruciating before. He used to pace, get on his phone, watch the floor numbers. But elevators come when they want to come. So, he pretended he was patient. He'd act like a patient person, standing there without fidgeting, chatting with the receptionist even though he was lit dynamite on the inside.

At work he acted like it was no big deal, he made himself hold back on swearing and carrying on when the market made some weird, volatile jump.

"I'm still not feeling it," he kept telling me. "I'm the world's most impatient guy, it's never going to change."

"Stop listening to that Old Story voice," I told him. "Keep faking it."

And then one day, he went out to lunch with his girlfriend, who is always trying to operate on his time frame. He eats very fast. When he was done eating, he got up to leave, and she said, "Honey, I haven't finished my tea." He sensed it was an opportunity to practice patience. At first he sat down through willpower. "Take your time, finish your tea." But while he sat there, he noticed that he was enjoying it, he started to relax for the first time in he didn't know how long. He found that he was loving watching his girlfriend at the café, got a kick out of the people around him, he stopped thinking about work, he stopped concerning himself with "what's next?" He was able to be with her, and it was nice. He doesn't usually call and tell me when he's made progress in his New Story work, but that day he called and said, "I just did it. I didn't just act it. I really did it. I felt patient." It was true, he just took one step in the process of being infinitely patient. It felt small on the outside, but from the inside it felt like making the best investment of the year.

Have you ever seen the movie *My Life*? In it, Michael Keaton finds out that he has just 4 months to live and won't even get to see his child born. He wants to teach her about life, and one lesson is about how to exhibit confidence when walking into a room. So he makes a video of all the ways one can enter a room: looking down, bubbly and smiley, serious and quiet. He finally settles in on walking in with shoulders back, head up, eyes alert, and making contact with each person there.

His message? To act on the outside the way you want to feel on the inside. When you fake it, when you have the courage to be a little bit uncomfortable and playact who you really want to be, the effect is miraculous, you start to be what you are projecting.

SESSION TIP

The Big But: But I am afraid I will feel like a total phony when I do this, and everyone will know I'm faking it! What if I just fake it forever and never actually make it?

Try This On For Size: In fact, most of the time we *are* just faking it. How many times have you asked someone how they were and didn't actually want to know? How many times have you felt lousy and said "Good!" when someone asked you how you were?

We have a lot of practice faking it, and while most people you meet will take how you act and what you say at face value, they won't spend the time wondering whether you are what you say you are. And what's the alternative? Would you rather fake being a good sport, or show your bad sportmanship? Would you rather pretend you feel like you are flying at work, or show the workplace that you feel like a loser? Faking it is just practice for actually feeling it. Act like an Oscar-nominated star and go for it! At the very least, you'll trick your brain into believing it and find yourself firing some feel-good neurotransmitters!

CHAPTER 33

Training for the Unthinkable

It wasn't raining when Noah built the ark.

—HOWARD RUFF

There's a hard rain gonna fall.

—BOB DYLAN

Change before you have to.

—JACK WELCH

For much of my life as a coach, I felt like a fraud. A fraud in the sense that almost everything I said felt like a retread of the successful people I'd studied. I turned all of the people I'd read into my personal coaches and used their ideas to become better.

When I entered tennis tournaments, I tested all their tools. I was my own personal experiment. But I was always unsure of myself. I would do Jim Loehr's mental toughness program, but I'd never really do it to the level I thought I should. I would start to have some successes and then I would admonish myself for letting go of the discipline. I felt like I was still too controlled by results and what people thought of me. Despite this, over time I went from being a strong athlete who lost most of the time to being a multiple national champion, a world champion, a Hall of Famer. I coached people to hit great golf shots, kick field goals, audition in front of American Idol judges, invest a million bucks of their clients' money, communicate with a parent, friend, spouse. But there was always a little voice in my head that said, *fraud*. Maybe my success was happening, not *because* of these tools, but despite them. Maybe I just played enough and was lucky enough to simply improve.

What I didn't know then was that regardless of my own Old Story that I wasn't enough, I was training for the unthinkable. Stay positive. One step, one step. Bring your angels and leave your judges. Stay in the present. Fire hope-filled emotions. Incinerate the past. Smile. Reduce reactivity to what others say or think about me. Focus. Love adversity. Turn frustration into challenge. Write a list of gratitudes. Sit in silence. Maintain freedom from mental anguish. Stay detached from creating right/ wrong dynamics . . . and on and on. I ate right. I developed new stories and read them daily. I kept a chart to hold myself accountable. Still, I thought I wasn't doing enough.

Until *bam,* in September, 2007 it was *game on*. Not a tennis match. Not a conversation with an employer. Not a client in need. No, this was the real deal. The hardest match of my life. Carol, my wife of thirty years, my soulmate, got devastating news. She had breast cancer. This match would be life changing.

This was not about a ranking in tennis, more or less revenue at work, or saying the right or wrong thing in the moment.

This would be the ultimate test of all of the mental training. This would be where I would put to use all I had been saying to myself and to others. This would be about dealing with a huge life situation, not a game. And I realized that all the training for tennis was never for tennis, it was for Carol, standing with her as she faced illness, pain, and found courage, worked through despair, and sought joy.

It was tough. There were moments and days that I failed, where I was impatient at the doctor's office or lost my focus at work or pleaded with the universe to stop putting us through this awful experience. Most days, though, even the very darkest of Carol's final three months, three years after the diagnosis, the tools, the practice, kept me in an effective state. For the first time I started to feel that the words that I was giving my clients and students were mine. I was no longer a parrot passing on information. I was a living example of the tools I'd been practicing.

What's odd now, looking back, is that I always thought I was doing it for tennis and work, I never considered for a moment that I was training for life, for how to be a better person in my life. And once in a while when I was talking to a friend or a colleague, to my daughters or Carol's relatives, I would realize all the work that I'd done was really about preparing me for this. Everything I was teaching had to do with something that I couldn't even imagine.

When Carol passed away I went through the most massive change, but I was able to face it, learn from it, come out on the other side, because I had trained with far lesser things: tennis points, money, what we lose in the market. Of course,

I would give all that training back for her to be alive, but thank goodness I had that training at my disposal.

In 2008, Amanda Ripley, a reporter for *Time* wrote a book called *The Unthinkable: Who Survives When Disaster Strikes—and Why*. Half of all Americans have been affected by a disaster of some kind, and in this book she tries to bring light into civilization's darkest moments. Why do we freeze in the middle of a fire? How can we override this instinct? Why does our sight and hearing change during a terrorist attack? Why are most heroes men? In the book she discusses the science of how human fear circuits work and why our instincts misfire, and how we can change that. The lesson is this: change before you have to. Ergo the flood comes and we have no ark. Anticipate. Prepare. Train. You never know when the next flood is coming. Everybody is going to face something difficult in their life.

After Carol died, I went back to work several weeks later with a message for all: Train now. Train hard. You never know what is around the corner. You never know what life will throw at you. Somehow we don't think that we have to prepare for the greatest difficulty we are going face. We are all masters of denial; God forbid that one of your kids is going to get badly injured in a car accident, a parent could die or you or someone you love could be struck with an awful illness. The tragedy will change your perspective. The tools are your training ground for that tragedy. When things are going pretty well, we tend to be complacent about training our attitude and spirit, but that's the time to keep practicing. When things start to go south in some area of our lives, we won't have the time or inclination to train. The biggest lesson is that we will all be faced with life-changing experiences. It could be the loss of job, money, our home, illness or death.

None of us gets through life without an experience that can change us forever. You are always training for the unthinkable. I am not a pessimistic person, but you have to realize now that something really bad can come.

Now it's nearly six years later, and I look back on that period as the best period of my life. Not the happiest, of course, but as the period with the most texture: love, devotion, caring for Carol and others, family, freedom from self-judgment, living in the present, learning, perspective and personal growth. All that training that I had stumbled into got me ready for this gigantic challenge. Losing Carol is not likely to be the last.

Train now before tragedy hits so you can deal with your life like a champion.

SESSION TIP

The Big But: But this feels pretty morbid to me. I'm training for something horrible to happen? Isn't that sort of like thinking pessimistically?

Try This On For Size: The unthinkable is actually on the periphery of our thoughts all the time. We are constantly faced with the horrible task of keeping those thoughts at bay. We know that we are all human, and that events that are beyond our control will certainly happen, traumatic in scope. Overcoming this obstacle gives you a pragmatic answer to those unconscious thoughts and some sense of security. It lets you know that, when it arises, you will be ready for it.

CHAPTER 34

Nuggets on the Path

> Rules of the road: What appears to be a
> detour may be the most important leg of
> the journey.
>
> —JUDY CANNATO

> We're so engaged in doing things to
> achieve purposes of outer value that we
> forget the inner value. The rapture that is
> associated with being alive is what it is all
> about.
>
> —JOSEPH CAMPBELL

In the book *The Myth of Zen and the Art of Archery*, Eugen Herrigel, a German professor, had an opportunity to teach in Tokyo and jumped at it as a chance to study Zen. At the outset, all the teachers rejected him because, "It was hopeless for a European to attempt to penetrate into this realm of spiritual life unless he began by learning one of the Japanese arts associated with Zen."

Because Herrigel has experience in rifle shooting, he thought the art of archery seemed suitable. At first he thought he was practicing to get a bull's-eye. But his master let him know that, "The right art is purposeless, aimless!" In other words, to hit the target you must not think about hitting the target, or even that it exists.

What happened as a result of this practice was far more miraculous than hitting a bull's- eye. Herrigel found focus, absolute presence, that place of total freedom where the busy mind quiets and there's peace; he experienced that wild, almost blissful feeling of pulling the arrow out of the sleeve, loading the arrow to the bow string, withdrawing the bow, and then the dynamic moment when he would open his fingers and release the arrow. Just as there is a dynamic moment in nature, the moment right before the fruit falls from the tree or the moment before the flower petals open, there is the moment where the archer lets go and discovers life as is needs to be lived. The paradox was that too much attention on the bull's-eye, created internal tension that interfered with getting the bull's-eye, the perceived victory. He may hit the bull's-eye; he may not. But regardless his journey was beautiful, inspiring, life changing.

That is the nugget on the path.

I read this during my sophomore year at Michigan, and it may have been one of the first books that awakened me out of a deep sleep. My grades began to improve as I took my focus off the grades and entered a new state. By the time I graduated, I'd gone from a 2.8 to a 3.75 in my final semester. I watched others memorize like crazy to get a high grade. Maybe they scored highly but they retained very little and never got the high of experiencing the learning for its intrinsic value. When we are looking into the future for results and goals, we cannot see those nuggets. This is why we often lose the lesson that is right in front of it while we are on the path.

My work with traders and analysts still draws on that book. It also draws from Mihaly's theory of the autoletic personality: performing acts because they are intrinsically rewarding, rather than to achieve external goals. I teach the traders and athletes that goals are one path and the intrinsic value of the action that gets you there is another path. These paths run like a helix, weaving back and forth, crossing each other but always moving forward. The result? They enjoy their lives while also reaching goals. One is not mutually exclusive of the other.

In Eckhart Tolle's book *A New Earth*, he says we are human beings who spend 99.9 percent of our lives accomplishing tasks: working, exercising, being parents, going to the cleaners, eating, but we don't spend a lot of time just being. We are so focused on doing, we ignore the fact that it feels good to exercise, even if you don't gain a ton of muscle; a strawberry tastes great on the tongue, even if you are eating it because it's on your diet; and it's actually fun to sing along to the radio while you are on the way to the cleaners.

Ultimately, we are all moving toward our own inevitable mortality. That's really the last bull's-eye, and we need to enjoy and maximize the nuggets on the path to there. It doesn't have to be as serious as the German professor going to Japan to learn Zen and feeling the intrinsic pleasure of drawing a bow.

In 2014 I was selected to go to Croatia to play for the USA on the senior Davis Cup team. The final weekend conflicted with Tennis Congress, a very special event which brings elite coaching to recreational athletes. As a board member and the head of the mental coaching component, I didn't want to miss it. Play for the USA. Teach at Tennis Congress. Croatia. Tucson. I was ambivalent. I wanted to do both.

The teaching gods intervened. In mid-August I tore a calf muscle. Davis Cup not an option. So I made my plans to go to Tucson to teach the storytelling model to 300 eager students. Three days of deepening my presentations, giving to others, and building my brand. During this time I was also in the process of trying to let go of a lifetime in New York and making the decision to move to Colorado, one that was filled with uncertainty.

On the first day there I went to a stretching class led by the brilliant Phil Wharton. When the class was over I told him that I was recovering from a calf tear and he told me to hop onto his table for a treatment. While he was working on me I was aware that he was moving my leg to a certain position and then just waiting. Not really pushing the stretch. I asked what he was doing and he said he was just waiting. Waiting until he felt the right moment. The moment that I was willing to let go . . . and then he would stretch it. He said that he was just trusting that my muscle would trust him as long as he didn't force things. When he said that, my muscle just relaxed. It had trusted him.

When the session ended I got off the table and had a sense of peace. I went back to my room and told Jo Ann, "We can go to Boulder." What was different? I felt the trust. The trust that everything would work out. That I had always found the way to work things out in my life. All I needed to do was trust.

So, you see, I went to Tennis Congress to teach and grow my brand and I came away with the most beautiful nugget on the path. Trust.

I tore a calf muscle and ended up moving to Boulder.

Having experienced some large changes in my life over the last 10 years—from changing my career from tennis teacher to business and life coaching, getting a new hip, losing my beloved wife, re-growing my life, falling in love again, getting married again, and moving to Boulder, I've learned something, something I thought I already knew: life is short. Don't waste a day. If you work at it maybe you won't waste an hour or, even, a moment. Everything that happens, happens for a reason. What looks like a boulder on the path, interfering with a steady journey is there to move you to the next place. What looks like a detour is often a golden nugget on your path. Look for them. Save them. They are, when you look back, what makes the journey to your New Story even sweeter.

SESSION TIP

The Big But: But if I lose the goal and the horizon point and just start noticing the power of what happens along the path, I will never get where I am actually going.

Try This On For Size: Losing track of the goal is the whole point of noticing nuggets on the path. The common saying, "A watched pot never boils" is very apropos. When you focus on your goal and endpoint, for a long time it won't seem to be getting any closer. We need other "hits" to get us in the direction of our goal. When the path there contains golden nuggets, we are far more likely to stay on that path.

CHAPTER 35

What's Really Important?

Dream as if you'll live forever, live as if
you'll die today.

—James Dean

Our lives are defined by opportunities,
even the ones we miss.

—F. Scott Fitzgerald

Last year a 35-year old portfolio manager, loved by all, dropped dead of a heart attack two days after Christmas. His death shook up the entire firm. To the last person these men who lived their lives by the dollar suddenly realized their concerns about PNL were small compared to losing their lives. The thoughts that their spouses or children could lose them made them take time to hug them and tell them how much they loved them. They began to leave the office earlier. Some put their smartphones away before walking home. Eating better and taking breaks during the day moved up the to-do list. Sitting in front of their screens non-stop was no longer the norm.

The founder of the firm was among the most affected. He's always surrounded by people, but at the memorial service, he sat alone, sad, shocked, making promises to himself so that his three kids would have him around for a long time. His priorities—his sense of what is truly important was changing.

It is common that these realizations don't last forever. Many of us deny that this could happen to us. Work and life as it was begins to take over again. *It won't happen to me. He had a bad family history. He ate poorly. He over-exercised with a weak heart. Not me. I need to focus on work and keep putting up good numbers for the investors.*

And then another tragedy hit, one of the most well-liked guys in the firm lost his dad to cancer. Their last months together had been a journey of love and devotion as the father went through chemo, radiation, weakened bones, loss of focus, and the realization that the end was coming.

The funeral was held on a Monday. Monday is the day traders and analysts set up their portfolios for the week, the absolute worst day to be out of the office. But funerals don't get scheduled around business commitments, and almost everyone in the firm came to the funeral. For their friend and his family. And also for themselves. They all have parents. They stopped and thought, "This could have been my father." One of the top performers in the firm told me he'd called his dad that morning. "And when he answered I cried. I cried just because he answered the phone and I heard his voice."

As for the son whose dad had died, he sat shiva, a Jewish tradition of stopping regular life for several days and letting others take care of you. It is a special time, and it allows for the deceased family to spend time reflecting on the good life that had just ended. For the good memories to flow. To feel connected to each other and to oneself. When his colleagues asked him when he was coming back to work, he said, "I don't know. It doesn't seem to matter right now as much as being with my family and my memories." Some asked what about his stock positions, which he always watched so carefully. "I am not thinking about it. It is only money." He was in a state of awareness about what was really important.

Sure work is important. It pays the bills. It provides security. It allays fear of the future. It buys us food and shelter and lots of good stuff. But what really matters? Life matters. Living matters. Family matters. Love and devotion matter. Feeling a connection to others matters. Your mission matters. When Jeff Bezos, the founder of Amazon, was asked why he left a lucrative job as a hedge fund trader to start Amazon.com in his garage, he said, "I call it a regret minimization framework." He went on to say he projected himself into his 80s and asked what regrets he had about his life. We often don't think about the regrets we might have until we are faced with an illness, someone close to us dies, or we've undergone a trauma that makes us reevaluate everything in our lives. Your New Story constantly reminds you of what is important, so you don't have to wait for tragedy to do it for you.

I remember a guy at a research firm telling me "I will never again take anything for granted because my priest and his family, who lived down the block from me, died in a fire this weekend." But the end of the story is that he forgot. For just a while, he lived like everything he valued would be gone in a heartbeat, and then he went on thinking material objects, personal slights, money, and beating the competition were more important than love and connection.

In order to live a life of regret minimization, you have to live as though your 90-year-old self were looking over your shoulder, constantly reminding you of what you'll regret when you are too aged and infirm to do much. It means greeting the ones you love, focusing on them, spending time with them, as though they could be gone in a heartbeat. They could.

So with these experiences happening in the world around him, the founder of the firm, getting a sense of what is really important, pulled out his New Story: *I am infinitely patient, eager to consider others' wishes as well as my own. Every day I wake up committed to be better, in some way, than I was yesterday. I put my ideas about positive change on my daily to-do list. Each day I do something to make a meaningful difference in somebody's life. Sometimes it might just be calling someone by his or her name or appreciating what someone has done, whether it be for me or for someone else. I am eternally grateful, appreciating all the parts of my life. I value each day as a gift and share my gratitudes with others. I make great decisions every day that keep me healthy. Aging has no chance against me as I am a master of managing my body through exercise, eating, drinking, and sleeping. I am persistent in my work toward becoming the very best that I can be.* He began again to use the tools to move toward it.

Why do we need a tragedy to find out what's important? What's important needs to be running below the surface at all times. In order to do that, we need to find the heightened place where your morality is, where your days are numbered, where the world as you know it could end. And while that sounds morbid, it actually brings to the surface those things that are most important about life, the sweet things, the kiss before you leave the house, helping your son with his art project instead of answering that text, risking the safety of a job you don't love so that you can finally, finally, make your dreams come true. Your New Story is all about what is really important and the more we take the steps toward living it, the happier we will be when we look back.

SESSION TIP

The Big But: But what I think is important changes day to day, and sometimes moment to moment. I can't decide which thing is more important than the next; what if I choose the wrong thing?

Try This On For Size: There's no right or wrong to what's important. Sometimes in the moment, we want to spend time with our family but we have to move forward on a project that's under deadline. In that case focusing on what's important may be this: "I am doing this so that I can provide for my family." This turns the attention on what's really important: family, love, relationships.

When we keep that larger picture as our bull's eye, we create tremendous value in all that we do.

CHAPTER 36

Back Stories

Love and compassion are necessities, not
luxuries. Without them humanity cannot
survive.

—Dalai Lama

A couple of weeks ago, I sat down with Aidan, a tall, handsome
former soccer goalie with an energy that fills a room. He's a
software engineer who develops programs that benefit kids with
learning challenges. He's a huge success in his field and so excited
about life, he talks fast; so fast it can be hard to keep up with him.

We had just hiked up to Flagstaff in Boulder and were sitting
overlooking the plains, talking about his kids, his love for his
parents and brothers, his career, and the oppportunities his work
has granted him.

During the course of our conversation, he brought up some
challenges he was having with his wife. Because he came from
a modest background, he's really grateful that he's financially

secure. He loves his family and doesn't feel like there's much to worry about. "I'm grateful all the time, but my wife worries non-stop." When I asked what she worried about he said, "Everything! We're not saving enough, the house we just bought is too small for the new baby, she needs to be with the kids all the time when they're not in school because the world is unsafe. No matter how much I do for her or how much I make, it feels like she's never grateful. She can't just relax and enjoy life." As his words came stumbling out, it became clear that in fact Aidan's marriage was in pretty big trouble. He wasn't sure he wanted to live with someone who had what he felt like was a negative view of the world. But he loved her, she was a great mom, capable, strong, beautiful, personable, a great partner in so many ways.

Finally he turned and looked at me, and I could see the pain in his eyes. "So, how to bridge that gap?" he asked me. "Between wanting to enjoy her and feeling like she's just too different and I should find a partner who is happier, more joyful, and grateful about what we have?"

Really, Aidan was only missing one key ingredient in his marriage: compassion for his wife's backstory. When I asked him about her upbringing, he thought a minute. "Well," he said, slowly, "she is Croatian, and she had to live through the war in Bosnia before her family was finally able to escape. They lost everything and had to start over from scratch. A cousin that she was close to was killed. They never found his body or his grave. All her life she and her family have worried that everything could be taken away in a moment."

I nodded. And then I told him that famous Stephen Covey story about the man who gets on the subway at the end of a long day of work. Four wild, noisy kids are kicking up a racket, and the man can't get a moment's peace. The man with him is doing nothing about it. "Are those your kids?" the man asks the father. "Oh yes they are."

"Well can't you control them?" he asks. The man apologized, saying that he hadn't really noticed because they had just been to the hospital, where their mother was very ill.

The man on the train instantly shifted from annoyed to understanding.

Aidan has a backstory, too. He was brought up in a modest home, where they valued being grateful for all they had. He felt safe and free of worry. And now that he has even more than he had then, he's doubly grateful, he's on top of the world.

By cultivating understanding and compassion for his wife's backstory, he will be able to say "I understand you" when his wife's attitude about life gets negative.

The next time Aidan called, he told me, "That was a total blast to my brain. I'm not only seeing Ana differently, I'm seeing the whole world differently. I'm forgiving people left and right, people I've been critical of for years. I feel so in love with my wife." He told his kids about the backstory and when the kids would complain that mommy was being impatient, he would ask them "what's happening with mommy that she might be acting differently?" And they would say, "Her backstory is that she is eight months pregnant." And they would understand.

Everyone has back stories. Not everyone knows that they and others have these stories. If you know about them you can be more understanding in your interactions with others. If you are aware that you have back stories you will find it easier to change your outer behavior, your way of doing what you do. What you are basically doing is cultivating compassion, which has become very hip these days. Compassion has a twitter page, Stanford University is establishing a compassion center at their school of Medicine, the Dalai Lama is famous for it, and Leslie Jamison's popular essay, "Effort is Not the Enemy of Compassion", in *The Atlantic* last spring was celebrated widely on the Web.

Researchers have found that compassion or being willing to understand others' backstory is an incredible tool, it speeds up recovery from disease and even lengthens our life spans. This may be because our well-being is boosted when we widen our perspectives about people beyond our own story about them. Depression and anxiety are linked to a preoccupation with the self. When you think about where someone else is coming from, your mood lifts, you feel energized, and you've usually gotten a better perspective on your own circumstances, too.

One of my buddy's daughters was having a tough time with a college roommate. She'd hide in the closet, whispering to him on the phone that her roommate was erratic and odd, sulking one minute and hysterical the next. She complained it was impossible to live with her. During parents' weekend he was sitting on her roommate's bed, waiting for his daughter to get ready for dinner and noticed a pill container on the night table. He's a doctor and knew right away the medication was for bipolar disorder.

Knowing this backstory helped his daughter move from annoyance and dislike to compassion and understanding. She learned something about her own backstory too: she had high expectations of others. The backstory is not only a pathway toward better relationships with others, it's can also be a key to understanding ourselves.

When we aren't willing to contemplate another's backstory,

we actually get stuck in the stories they are acting out. We get stuck with them. The moment we understand that, Hey! You have a backstory (sometimes called an Old Story!) and I have a backstory, we're all in this together, you tend to get unstuck from your limited prejudices or biases around someone else's actions. You may not know why the guy got on the subway with four kids and let them run wild, but try to imagine there might be a backstory in there, something that, if you learned it, would instantly pull at your heart strings. Connect with people, ask them the stories behind their actions. If they don't know? Imagine that they must have a very valid reason for acting the way they do, have what I call "blind" compassion for them. It's a lot like blind faith and it can help make your world a much happier place.

SESSION TIP

The Big But: But when I think of someone's backstory, aren't I just making excuses for their bad behavior?

Try This On For Size: Bad behavior is often perpetuated by how we relate to someone and what we think of them. Part of breaking the cycle of bad behavior is changing how we react to it. So, if you begin to see that behind every action is a backstory, you will act differently toward that person, and they will tend to respond accordingly. So, the question is: Do you want to feel better? Do you want better relationshps? Backstory can be the answer.

CHAPTER 37

Just Show Up: No Magic

Hope begins in the dark, the stubborn
hope that if you just show up and try to do
the right thing, the dawn will come.
You wait and watch and work: you don't
give up.

—Anne Lamott

Julian and I first met to discuss working together at a beautiful San Fransisco yacht club he had recently joined. He needed a spot to keep a recently purchased boat. He told me right away that he didn't even know why he had bought this boat. A friend had hit some financial slide so Julian took the boat off his hands. It wasn't the only thing he talked about that day that started with "I don't know why I . . ."

He was a prototype stock trader. Wiry, fast talking, short

bursts of attention, moving from subject to subject. It was a challenge to follow but I waited for the underlying themes to rise to the surface.

His life, he told me, felt like driving a car 170 miles per hour. He was afraid that if he hit the brakes, he would lose control and crash. He couldn't sleep at night. He wasn't spending meaningful time with his kids or wife even though his office was five minutes from home. He didn't know why he was still working at this large financial firm where he had been for eight very successful years. He was paranoid that they were trying to get rid of him despite his contributing over $50 million a year in their annual revenues. He didn't feel supported. He thought that he should be starting his own hedge fund so that he would have equity and make a bigger percentage of the returns that he put up when investing capital.

Over the first few months we worked on his story. Who do you want to be? What kind of person? Who in the business is a positive role model for you? What he needed to do was create consistency, to show up for his New Story in a way he hadn't been showing up for his kids, his wife, or himself. It helped Julian that there were a lot of tools to keep his mind occupied, and he did keep showing up. He used *Kaizen*. He asked the *Can*. He spoke positively to himself. He stayed in the present. Once he felt that he had slowed down from 170 miles per hour and could see the road in front of him, we began to talk strategy for starting his own business. The Julian hedge fund.

His first step was that he needed to show up for himself, not just talk about what he wanted for himself but actually show up and ask for it. He went to the head of the big financial firm he worked for to present a plan and see if he could get the firm to be his partner in the new fund. The firm would pay expenses, provide capital, take a smaller piece of the pie, and approve outside capital. Those revenues would be Julian's and his investors alone. The firm wouldn't get a cut. They jerked him around, keeping his questions at bay, rescheduling meetings. But Julian kept showing up with his bottom line. This is what I want. He kept asking in a patient, even way, presenting his research and speaking up for himself. Last week he sat with the head of the firm. He was ready to have his plan rejected, but he showed up anyway. The big head said, "Okay, let's do it. You can do what you want here and we will be your partner."

Julian called me, a little stunned. "What do I do now?" he asked. "How do I turn this into a reality? I don't know how to set up a $2 billion hedge fund. Should I even do this?"

The trepidation about change was starting to move him into his Old Story of not showing up. Doubt, uncertainty and fear were creeping in. "After all," he said. "I'm making big money just by being one of the analysts."

"Keep showing up," I told him. "No magic, just show up."

So he did. He showed up by doing some research about how much money he would need to launch, he showed up to lunch with a buddy who had started a similar fund, he showed up to talk to a junior analyst who had been CFO at another hedge fund so knew about the numbers, and then he showed up to a first conversation with the "big head" about the expenses that the big fund would pay. He kept showing up, every step of the way. Every time he showed up, asked the questions, did the research, talked to the "big head," and felt calmer.

Sometimes when we show up, the results aren't that great. Abe Lincoln went to war a captain and returned a private. Afterward, he was a failure as a businessman. As a lawyer in Springfield, he was too impractical and temperamental to be a success. He turned to politics and was defeated in his first try for the legislature, again defeated in his first attempt to be nominated for the U.S. Congress, defeated in his application to be commissioner of the General Land Office, defeated in the senatorial election of 1854, defeated in his efforts for the vice presidency in 1856, and defeated in the senatorial election of 1858. But he kept, kept, kept showing up. Finally he became one of the most influential leaders this country has ever seen.

In *The War of Art,* Steven Pressfield talks about how new writers tend to say they are going to start the day at 9 AM, but that turns into 9:15, then 9:30. Professionals, he says, show up every day. They don't knock off at 2:00 because it isn't going well—they work. This is the same with your New Story, you wrote it, you know that's who you want to be, now every time there is an opportunity to live it, however small, however piddly or unimportant it seems to be, show up. When Carol was sick, a breast cancer foundation wanted to honor her as their courageous person of the year. She turned them down saying, "I am not courageous, I just get up each day and try and get through the day in as good a way as possible. That is not courage. It is just showing up."

Show up for yourself, for your family, for your work, for your mission. Remember that Babe Ruth hit the most home runs the very same year that he had the most strike-outs; he kept showing up at home plate, he kept trying.

Keep showing up.

SESSION TIP

The Big But: But I want the magic. That's why I'm working toward the New Story!

Try This On For Size: In the story of the golden fleece, Jason has to yoke fire-breathing bulls, slay dragons and sail rough seas. While he does have magic at his disposal, it is the fact that he shows up that eventualy wins him the fleece; the magic only winds up getting him in trouble. Showing up is the most under-rated action we can take. It may not have the pop and shine of other sessions, but showing up is simple to do, and is one of the fastest ways to living your New Story.

CHAPTER 38

The Gift of Adversity

The greatest glory in living lies not in never falling, but in rising every time we fall.

—Nelson Mandela

Adversity introduces a man to himself.

—H. L. Mencken

It is during our darkest moments that we must focus to see the light.

—Aristotle Onassis

Life is not about waiting for the storms to pass . . . it's about learning to dance in the rain

—Vivian Green

This is not just a human potential book, it's a story: the story of a man who thought he had it all, and then lost the love of his life to cancer and in the midst of that tragedy found a sliver of dazzling light, a crack that became a doorway, that turned out to be the portal to living the best stories of our lives.

In many ways, this is Carol's book, she is the beating heart. The adversity we faced is absolutely everywhere in the white space. It is the current that runs beneath the book's practical approach. That challenge gave me the certainty to say that yes, change is possible, change is lasting, change is what life is about, there is strength in fear, despair can grow joy, life goes on, and you can be defeated by it or you can grow bigger from it. Carol's illness was the vehicle that showcased every tool I'd ever used and validated that they really did work. Carol's illness taught me the story of blue skies behind the clouds, gratitude during difficult times, doing the work even when things go south, of walking the walk, discovering how high we can jump, of love and devotion, living in the present, optimism, and how adversity builds strength. It also gave me the sweet message that the opportunity to Live the Best Story of Your Life is there for each of us, and we don't have to lose someone to know it.

Anyone who ever came into contact with Carol loved her. We were at a party once and someone who had never met her before pegged her as an edifier, a person who, despite being an extraordinary person, managed to make those in their presence feel that they were the most special, unique person in the whole world. After she died, I received letters from people from around the world, people who had met her only once would tell me their life changed the day they met Carol. They were able to recognize things in themselves they had never seen before. She had the unique ability to see inside your goodness. She connected directly from her heart. Nobody had a laugh like hers. She lived in a state of joy. Imagine how lucky I felt that with all the people in the world that she met in her lifetime, she picked me to spend her life with.

ER visits, CT Scans, x-rays, IVs, pain meds. The disease was a tsunami, coming in slowly, building, and crashing with great force. Things changed by the hour. Her health was failing, and it was hard to say how long she would survive. Barring a miracle, it was going to happen. But Carol did not waver from the person that she was, a person who lived in the moment, who had compassion, who saw the can, who courted optimism. Sometimes she would apologize to me for bringing cancer into our lives, and I would deflect her apology by letting her know that through cancer I discovered feelings of adoration and tenderness at a depth that I would never have known. When she was so very sick and in the hospital during the final weeks, the doctors, nurses, and the staff who cleaned the rooms wanted to be with her. Even while she was in the midst of a devastating illness, she somehow took care of their spirits and made them feel special. Several of her doctors shared with me that the best part of their day was when they were able to come to her room and feel her love. These are people that tend to stay disconnected from their sick patients. She was amazing, continuing to give love to anyone who came into her sphere. In spite of being disengaged a large part of the time, all of the nurses wanted to be in her space.

On her footstone there is a Hebrew inscription: "*Ishat Rachamim*" (A woman of compassion). She showed us that even in the midst of adversity, tragedy, illness, crisis we do not have to live an Old Story, one of pain and can't and pessimism and fear. Carol was beautiful before the disease, and she was beautiful during the disease. She did not use the disease as a way to exhibit Old Story behavior or thinking. She proved to me and everyone around her that you can continue to live a New Story, even in the face of the worst calamity imaginable. Even in the face of death.

This is not easy. Adversity is a fierce teacher. It hits us when we least expect it. In 2005, I won the World Championships in Perth, I'd just starting working as a coach for hedge funds and loved it, I was moving away from teaching tennis and felt this incredible freedom and exploration of something new. I was feeling extraordinary for having defaulted the year before because of Yom Kippur, we were happy, secure financially, our daughters had gotten married. I remember coming home from Perth and doing a slideshow of our time there. The music I chose was "These are the Days," by 10,000 Maniacs. What I didn't know was that Carol was sick. We didn't know it was cancer. I thought I was the luckiest man in the world.

How wrong I was.

Life can get the drop on you like that. Someone dies, you are the victim of a crime, your spouse asks for a divorce, your house burns down, and you can find yourself right back in the Old Story again, rather than living your New Story. The best way to remedy this is to see what a fantastic gift adversity can be, to not crumble under the weight of it.

Adversity isn't necessarily illness or death. After his first audition, Sidney Poitier was told by the casting director, "Why don't you stop wasting people's time and go out and become a dishwasher or something?" It was at that moment, recalls Poitier, that he decided to devote his life to acting. At the age of 21, French acting legend Jeanne Moreau was told by a casting director that her head was too crooked, she wasn't beautiful enough, and she wasn't photogenic enough to make it in films. She took a deep breath and said to herself, "Alright, then, I guess I will have to make it my own way." After making nearly 100 films her own way, she received the European Film Academy Lifetime Achievement Award in 1997. Fred Smith, the founder of Federal Express, received a "C" on his college paper detailing his idea for a reliable overnight delivery service. His professor at Yale told him, "Well, Fred, the concept is interesting and well formed, but in order to earn better than a "C" grade, your ideas also have to be feasible." F. W. Woolworth was not allowed to wait on customers when he worked in a dry goods store because, his boss said, "he didn't have enough sense." Beethoven. For a musician to lose his hearing is the greatest possible misfortune. Yet, despite the inevitable frustration, it didn't stop Beethoven from composing some of the most sublime pieces of music in the history of the world.

I don't recommend going out and looking for adversity, but we don't have to, it finds us. So the question really is, once it does, what are the best ways of dealing with adversity and what can we extract from it that's going be beneficial going forward?

First of all, adversity has the downside of leading to mental anguish. Your thoughts tend to spin, you forget to write your gratitudes, pessimism takes over, you are no longer living in the present. A very close friend, a psychologist, who is very in touch, is disciplined, and practices working on herself was visiting me after shiva for Carol ended. We were sitting on my deck and she was asking how I seemed to stay even-keeled during the last few years with Carol's illness, my two hip surgeries, and one of my grandchildren being born three months premature.

I told her that one of my missions was to be free of mental anguish. When feeling anguish, I would scan where I was in four different ways:

Was I in a state of acceptance or resistance?

Was I being non-judgmental or judgmental of myself, another or something?

Was I detached or attached to some position of right versus wrong?

Was I being forgiving or unforgiving of myself, of another, or of something that life had thrown at me?

Chances were that if I was experiencing mental anguish, I was on the wrong side of one or more of those questions. By asking the questions I was able to get some distance from whichever it was and was immediately freer of the anguish. I could also, then, clearly decide how I wanted to proceed with that kind of thinking. Did I want to let go or hold on to whatever was creating the anguish? Adversity can lead you to feel out of control, so giving yourself the choice is another step closer to freedom.

She laughed and said, "I should do that even when I'm not facing adversity." And she went home and began. That was in August. Six months later, we were on the phone and she was talking about feeling overwhelmed with a new grandchild, a husband who had surgery, a house renovation, and general life stuff. I asked about the mental anguish checklist? She'd forgotten it. A few months ago, life was going along smoothly for her and she stopped practicing. One day led to the next and before she knew it, she was experiencing anguish in little ways, but not so big that she remembered what had worked so well.

She is now back on the path, incrementally freeing herself of anguish. This is the experience of a person who is disciplined, committed and aware. It is easy for any of us to slip off of the path. It is so important to create a method of accountability that keeps us focused when adversity strikes.

We tend to be stronger and accomplish all things, much better when we are free of any negative state. And we are going to need strength when adversity strikes, so those questions can help us. As with other behaviors that may not appear to help us because the results don't necessarily occur instantly, people feel that it isn't worth investing the effort. We always tell stories to support our behavior even if the behavior is counterproductive. Just go through the list, practice when you aren't in adversity, with smaller situations, and it can help you exponentially when crisis hits.

During Carol's illness, I learned that the tools I'd been teaching and using on the court for years were golden, they could ride me through any situation. I found that I actually could stay with my New Story. I got to know myself in brand new ways, golden threads of resourcefulness I never knew were there.

It taught me that every time adversity hits, we can use it to find out how strong we are, to practice the New Story. Cultivating patience? Adversity is a great time to tone that muscle. Trying to be more loving? Adversity can be the challenge we need to test that love. Always, always ask yourself what you can learn from it. Put adversity to the test: Why are you here? To show me how committed I am? To test my ability to endure? To show me not to take it all for granted? To ask me what's important? If you have no idea what gifts adversity is bringing, tell yourself this: These heightened times of adversity are fodder for the best growth of my life, and I will be able to look back and know why this challenge hit.

My belief is that adversity is the fierce friend that chisels the rock so the hidden diamond can shine. Mihaly Csikszentmihalyi, who was held for a time in an Italian prison camp, survived, unlike many relatives and friends in Budapest who had been killed, and this experience had a big impact on his thinking and on how he chose to spend his life. "As a child in the war I'd seen something drastically wrong with how adults—the grown-ups I trusted—organized their thinking. I was trying to find a better system to order my life." It led him to go on to be one of the foremost leaders in the world on positive thinking.

It works the other way, too; adversity helps us get through life situations that are smaller in scope. My daughter Amy is doing a half triathlon soon. She told me she is worried and fearful about the open water swim. "Now that I am a parent, I am more cautious. I feel anxious. What should I do, Dad?" I told her that she has been training for difficult stuff all along, divorced parents, Carol getting sick, helping friends who were in dire straits. She has always been strong and even and supportive, a rock for her family and friends. Now she realizes that she can use what she has learned. That she can decide who she wants to be. That *she* can write the story and be a master of managing anxiety, to be courageous, to be worry free, and to make her middle name "calm." And she is ready for the open water swim.

Dr. Norman E. Rosenthal the world-renowned psychiatrist and bestselling author who wrote *The Gift of Adversity*, once told an interviewer, "From my years as a psychiatrist, I can tell you: imperfect marriages can be wonderful; imperfect children can bring boundless joy; an imperfect Christmas can be a time of giving and spiritual growth; that lousy vacation about which you will laugh and tell stories for years to come; and finally, realizing that your boss and job are imperfect will make you less grumpy every working day."

Often we don't look at adversity because it is too painful, but this is where the treasure is. If you use it to help you change, adversity is going to look like opportunity, it's not going to look like tragedy ever again. It's the gift you never knew you wanted. The gift you never thought you'd ask for. The best gift you could ever get.

SESSION TIP

The Big But: But there's a lot of grief in adversity; aren't I just in denial if I pretend it's a gift? Aren't I courting more adversity?

Try This On For Size: Seeing adversity as a gift doesn't necessarily mean that you like it or that it's a comfortable place to be. But the question remains: What will make you happier? Seeing the adversity as a horrible twist of fate or bad luck? Or remembering that adversity is actually a gold nugget in the path, sent to open up locked doors and show you even wider horizons?

CHAPTER 39

Look Back to See How Far You've Gone

Isn't it funny how day by day nothing changes, but when you look back everything is different.

—C. S. Lewis

I remember walking in Paris along the Seine from Notre Dame to the Eiffel Tower. The Tower stands alone with very little perspective of distance, and no matter how long I walked, it seemed as if the tower was getting no closer. But when I looked behind me to where I had been and how far I had come, I was able to see that I was making progress and, sure enough, I finally got there.

Sometimes it just feels like we are not getting anywhere, and at these times, you need to look back to see how far you have gone. We tend to mine the past for failures, for ways that we could have been better. But what about all the steps you took? Remember, you were once an itty bitty baby who could not feed or walk by yourself. You may have broken family legacies, whether emotional or otherwise, maybe you were the first to go to college, the first to have the sense to leave an unhappy marriage, maybe you raised a child, got your teaching license, started a business, maybe you failed at a business, maybe you faced illness and survived. These are all milestones, every single one of them, and we need to congratulate ourselves for them. We tend to forget that last year at this time, we hadn't seen as many sunsets, we hadn't loved our family for as many days—no matter how flawed that love sometimes felt, we hadn't taken the *kaizen* steps we needed to begin a project that is now begun.

Look back now, flip the page to the front of the book. Remember where you were when you stood in the bookstore flipping through the pages, or maybe someone gave it to you, and you weren't sure or you felt it was a sign, maybe you ordered it online, wherever you were; remember yourself then and think of yourself now. What has changed? A new perspective? A new horizon opened up? You are a different person now than you were then, change is inevitable, how are you different?

Every now and then, as you read your story and use your tools, think about where you were when you started your journey for the old to the new, from the you that you are leaving in the past to the new and better version of who you will be. The distance you have traveled will pump up your motivation for the next step; the New Story; the life of your wildest, happiest dreams.

SESSION TIP

The Big But: If I do that, then I'll begin to rest on my laurels. I'll relax, and I won't move forward. I'd rather keep charging ahead.

Try This On For Size: It's true; you *are* resting on your laurels. You deserve that once in a while. Just by the fact that you bought this book, I know you are not someone who rests on those laurels very often. You are interested in changing for the better, in living an even better story. Chances are, you can't help being that kind of person and spending some time looking at how far you have come will not sabotage that. Don't forget that nap time (Chapter 26) gives you the motivation and the energy to move on. So it's okay, relax and rest, you will soon find yourself charging ahead once again.

PART III

The Story
Still to Come

CHAPTER 40

Live the Best Story
of Your Life

Life is a game and you get to make the
rules.

—Bob Litwin

This book started with the idea that we all need a New Story about change. For too long, we have been sold a story that change is hard, that it takes a long time. But with storytelling, we see that change can be easy, fun, and it can happen in an instant.

What you need most in order to create instantaneous change is to become your own coach. I had a conversation the other day with a young mother I was working with, who was trying to decide whether to put her four-year-old into kindergarten. He is one month younger than the state deadline, so the decision falls to the parents.

"It's a big decision," she said. "If I hold him back, he will be the oldest in the class, and that could affect his motivation. He may not be challenged and that could stay with him throughout grade school, all the way through college. But if I push him, he'll be the youngest, and might be behind in social and mental skills. That could affect him forever. We just don't know what to do. It's such a big deal, and we don't want to make a mistake."

"Is that story working for you?" I asked her.

"Which story?"

"The 'it's a big decision' story. The 'really big deal' story."

"Well," she laughed, "I guess not, because we still can't figure out what to do."

"How about if you, just for a day or two, change the story to 'it is not that big a deal.'"

"But it is!" she protested.

"Well," I replied, "even if you don't believe that it isn't a big deal, what if you just told that story for a day or two? What do you have to lose? Maybe it will help you make the decision if you take the pressure off."

Two days later, I heard from Jessica. Almost as soon as we hung up, she'd seen very clearly that she had four possible outcomes: *I hold him back and he does fine*, or *I hold him back, and he doesn't. I move him forward and he does fine*, or *I move him forward, and he doesn't*. She knew they couldn't actually know what the outcome will be.

So how did she free herself up? We identified which part of her story was creating a block. The Old Story wasn't whether or not her son would be left behind or be too far ahead; those were areas she could not control. They were in the future. But there was one story she was telling herself that was in the now, and that's the story she could control: "It's a big deal."

Now she uses storytelling anytime she's in a spot that feels tough. "It is so simple," she told me recently. "And so powerful. Now, I'm a storyteller."

In writing this book, my intention was that you would gain the power to become your own coach, finding in your stories what isn't working. This came home to me when Eric, a huge producer at a financial firm who had written one New Story after another as a way to continue raising his game, was struggling with some physical issues. He was also trying to have a great finish to a tough year at work. He had a lot on his plate . . . and then his wife gave birth to his fourth son.

At 4:29 in the morning, he emailed me that he'd been up all night with his 18-month-old son. With everything going on in his life, from work to hip pain to trying to be there for his wife and his four kids, he hadn't been happy to get the tap on the shoulder to get up with his son. He was feeling frustrated, annoyed, and spent. But then he remembered all he needed was a New Story. Feeling inspired, he wrote his story:

I am super-dad. Some nights I will not sleep, some nights my kids won't sleep, but I will stay strong. I will stay patient because the sacrifice is all worth it in the end. The sleepless nights do not last forever, but love does. I don't know a father who hasn't had to put up with a kid waking up in the middle night; it is normal, it is natural. I will not let my kids down. I am a rock. Anything that is great is worth working hard for. A child's love is great and I will fight forever for that.

"I swear, Bob," he said, "after I wrote this I felt energized, excited, and blessed to be up with that little boy. He deserved nothing less than the best that I could be. I was a warrior. The New Story I wrote led me to instant change. I will always be a storywriter."

And, just from living this story, he was also juiced at work that day, fully present in the power of change.

We are all in different places on the journey to becoming master storywriters. At the beginning, it is an effort, and doubts pop up as much of the New Story feels like we are trying to fool ourselves into becoming something we are not. With practice, we become skilled and we can spot what part of our Old Story is tripping us up. Just like Eric, with the practice you get from these coaching sessions, you will be able to see your Old Story right away, write it down and move into your New Story in an instant.

Do Old Stories continue to pop up? Yes. I have been writing and living new stories for decades, and I still notice the stories that are holding me back. Any little wrinkle in my day, a feeling, attitude, reaction, thought that doesn't feel quite right . . . is an Old Story piece. But by now, I can quickly write a new one in my mind. And I do experience change. In an instant.

This book started with a story. A woeful story about where I was in my life in 2010, and how I wrote a New Story that inspired me to get to work. Five years later, I am living that story. The best story of my life.

But there is also the story of writing this book. Before this, I wrote journals—one-off blasts that went to my email list. I had never been able to turn being a writer into being an author. My story was this: I can't write a book.

It was a tired, Old Story.

I can't organize my thoughts. I can only write journals. I don't know what my themes are. I never finish anything I start. I am resistant. I am afraid of being judged. I am a fraud. Everything I write has already been written. I have no discipline. I want someone else to take my material and turn it into a manuscript.

I needed a New Story, but I started this book without ever writing my old and new stories. And I floundered. I wanted to do it so much, but couldn't get out of my own way.

So, once again, I decided to walk my talk. I wrote a New Story.

I am a master of creating order out of chaos. My journals are all connected with common themes. I always cross my finish lines. I battle the beast of resistance eagerly. I slay my inner critic when it surfaces. My voice speaks my truths. Discipline is my middle name. I can find the help I need to move through those pieces of book-building that feel like stumbling blocks. I am an author.

This has been a tough story for me to live as my Old Story popped up time and again.

I used my own private coaching sessions: I brought my angels and left my judges. I used Kaizen (one step at a time). I role-played with others. I danced with my beasts. I found my mission, my Big Why. I got the help I needed. I persisted.

And here I am, on the verge of completing a dream that I have had since 1975, when I pulled out that first composition book and wrote these words: "I am writing in this book those things that I have been saying to people on the tennis court. I don't know where these ideas and words come from, but they seem to help people move forward in their quest to improve. Each day, I forget a lot that I say. Just in case I want to remember, I will write these words each day."

I am in the final days of the book. The finish line is in sight. The Old Story of not finishing is fighting hard to stay alive. Each day I battle with my New Story voice. I fight the urge to just get it done rather than to see each day as shoshin moments, my own beginner mind. I fight to feel the joy of the experience, to stay focused, present, right here, right now.

I always cross my finish lines.

And now, finally, here is the book. I have lived the best story of my writing, and you have lived this journey with me.

You've gone through this book, written out your Old Stories, crafted your New Stories. You've read the distillations of 33 of the most powerful concepts in the field of human potential. You have gotten on the path, taken your first steps, created an inspirational new you. You've fought the beasts, and while you may have backslid, you got back up. Your Old Story is in the rearview mirror. You can hardly see it anymore. Your New Story is your new home. You find yourself wondering how you lived in that Old Story for so long.

From here on out, there will be parts of your New Story that will actually begin to become old. What this means is that you are on your way to another new, exciting story. You are one step closer to another New Story. Another new, improved version of you.

And the biggest part of your New Story will be: *I am a person who tells stories.*

I tell stories of the person I aspire to be. I tell stories of the person I know I can be, and I become that person.

And I always, always have the opportunity to write a brand New Story.

Acknowledgments

J ody and Amy, you have been there for so much of the ride. When it seemed like I had nothing left to give, you encouraged me. "We have lived the stories. It is time to write the book to share with the world what you have shared with us. Start with just one step and see where it takes you. You are right where you are supposed to be. You know it because that is where you are."

Jo Ann, you came into my life when it was dark. You brought blue skies. You have thrown me on your back and carried me to a new world filled with spontaneity, the mountains of Colorado, and incredible love and support. We continue to walk hand in hand as life unfolds effortlessly in front of us.

My "Big Chill" friends Susie Piser, John Gillette, and Peter Benedek, who propped me up daily during the dark times of Carol's illness. Tom Rosenthal, my oldest friend. We drank from the same well from the safe haven of Great Neck to similar spiritual awakenings. Michael Lieberman, who drew my first book out of me. It never left my desk but left me with a hole that I eventually needed to fill. Phil Wharton, for his ongoing guidance for my body and soul. PJ Simmons, who brought me back to the joy of teaching tennis and letting me do it my way. Ron

Paisner, who has been a scribe for my growth without ever writing a word, observing me through all the chapters of my life, steady, solid, always there, a brother to me.

My doubles partners Ray Lake, Kirk Moritz, Brian Cheney, Charlie Hoeveler, Lloyd Emanuel, and Jimmy Malhame: Each of you has taught me important lessons of how being a good person first can lead to big wins on the court. That the inner wins are more important than the trophies. You provided light for me on the path to competitive success that raised me as a coach for others.

Zim, JG, and Chas: Each one of you believed in me and gave me the opportunity to take the big jump from tennis to business coaching. You sensed my potential and took a chance on me, somehow knowing that I could make as big a difference in the office as much as on the playing field.

Wass and MM, you are two of my most enthusiastic supporters in the latest chapter of my life. You build me up by letting me help you and those in your lives. You get unlimited coaching for life.

To all of my students/clients over the last 45 years of coaching: A teacher learns by teaching others. Through your desire to raise your bar, your resistance, your questions, your attempts to follow through on my suggestions, and your feedback, you challenged me and always made me be better both for you and for me. You have inspired me to walk my talk, to never ask you to do what I would not do. Without you I would not have competed and discovered so many answers. You have all contributed to the storytelling model. Without you there would be no book.

Kelsey, Samantha, Brianna, and Laura. It was the work with you where the storytelling model grew to new levels. You did the work without question and as I saw your incredible results I knew that I needed to share the storytelling model with the world.

Jane, it continues to amaze me how we have loved, respected, and supported each other, unconditionally, for our whole lives. Mom and Dad would be proud of how we have lived their lessons of family. Mom, for your intuition and deep knowledge. Dad, for your competitive drive, your quiet confidence, you non-judgmental attitude, and for teaching me to play sports.

Dede Cummings, for appearing just at the right moment and selling my book. It is all about timing. Meg Donahue and Lisa Lorimer, for insisting that I meet your editor, Suzanne.

Suzanne Kingsbury, what can I say? When you told me to gather all of what I had written in my life—the journals, incomplete manuscripts, notebooks, notes on napkins and envelopes—and to put it in a big garbage bag and send it to you, it was a dream come true. You told me that you would move in with my writings and the book that needed to be written would write itself. You have come to know me as well as anyone in my life. You took me from being a writer to an author. Your belief in me kept me going when I wanted to stop. You helped me live my new story: "I am an author. I am a finisher." And you knew, during final editing, when I needed you most, to have dental surgery, so that I would cross the finish line on my own and take full ownership of my book. You knew that you could kick me out of the nest and I would fly. You are amazing.

Ryan Tumambing, Anna Krusinski, and Ryan Kennedy, for your extraordinary work, patience, and understanding during the editing process.

And to Andrew Flach and Hatherleigh Press for taking a chance on a new author who had strong views on every part of the process.

About the Author

Bob Litwin has spent over four decades using the New Story method to coach thousands of top athletes, coaches, Wall Street hedge funds, traders, and analysts to raise individual performance to extraordinary levels. A world tennis champion, Litwin is a #1 world ranked senior player, 18-time US National Champion, and an inductee into the Tennis Eastern Hall of Fame. He lives in Boulder, Colorado with his wife, Jo Ann.